Time to Pray!

Seasonal Prayer Services for Middle Grades

Time to Pray!

Patricia Mathson

ave maria press AmP Notre Dame, Indiana

Dedicated to students everywhere,

. . . .

that they may experience God's presence and love

. . . .

in their lives through prayer.

. . . .

Scripture quotations are from the *Today's English Version*, copyright © American Bible Society, 1966, 1971, 1976, 1992.

www.avemariapress.com

International Standard Book Number: 1-59471-020-1

Cover and text design by Katherine Robinson Coleman

Printed and bound in the United States of America.

Library of Congress Cataloging-in-Publication Data

Mathson, Patricia L.
   Time to pray! : seasonal prayer services for middle grades / Patricia Mathson.
      p. cm.
   ISBN 1-59471-020-1 (pbk.)
   1. Church year—Prayer-books and devotions—English. 2. Middle school students—Prayer-books and devotions—English. 3. Prayer—Catholic Church—Study and teaching. I. Title.

   BV30.M39 2004
   264'.0272—dc22

                              2004009934

Contents

Fall

Winter

Spring

Summer

Introduction

One of the most important things we do for students in our classrooms is help them learn to pray. We must help the students be people of prayer if they are to grow in faith and become everything that they were created to be.

Through prayer we lift up our hearts and our lives to God. We offer all that we have and all that we are to the God who created us and loves us. Prayer connects us with God who is Father, Son, and Holy Spirit. Prayer strengthens our relationship with God and with one another.

Prayer Services Involve Students in Prayer

Prayer services are a great way to draw students into prayer. Prayer services allow all the students to be actively involved in praying the responses and prayers. Students can proclaim the scripture readings and lead the intercessions. The prayer services in this book include many ideas for helping the students learn to pray in different ways. The prayers give the students words to express their thoughts and feelings to God. Prayer services encourage students to pray together for their needs and the needs of others.

Prayer Services Encourage Students to Live Their Faith

Enrichment ideas are included within the prayer services to encourage the students to live their faith. Ideas such as hearts for Jesus, the prayer chain, thank you leaves, the cross prayer, and others help students explore who we are called to be as disciples of Jesus Christ. The themes of the prayer services speak to what students are learning. The prayer services are geared for students in grades three to six, but can be easily adapted for other grade levels. These prayer services are for all God's children.

Prayer Services Call Students to Be Gospel People

Scripture is stressed in the prayer services since as Christians we are called to live the Word of God. The gospel is the heart of each prayer service. All the prayers and readings take their direction from the gospel message. The gospel readings are taken from all four gospels so that students explore all of the gospels. These prayer services help students learn that we are to live the values of the gospel in our lives. A listing of all the gospel passages used in these prayer services can be found at the back of this book.

Prayer Services Are for All Times and Places

The prayer services in this book can be used for prayer each week, each month, or each season of the church year. These prayer services can be prayed with individual groups of students, with several grade levels gathered for prayer or with an entire school or faith formation program. Families can be invited to celebrate these prayer services with the students. This book is a great resource for whole community catechesis, including parish programs, Catholic schools, Sunday programs, Vacation Bible Schools, family programs, or wherever students gather to give praise to God. Wherever there are students, there should be prayer.

Fall

The prayer services in the fall section will help get the year off to a great start for students, teachers, and catechists. These prayer services reflect what is going on in the liturgical year as well as in the lives of the students and the activities in the parish during September, October, and November.

The beautiful season of Ordinary Time calls us to live the teachings of Jesus Christ. The gospels that we hear proclaimed during this season call us to discipleship. They show us all what being followers of Jesus Christ is all about. Because Jesus Christ was the servant of all, we are called to serve others as he did. Ordinary Time is anything but ordinary. The word "ordinary" refers to the word "ordinal," marking the season as numbered time. Ordinary Time calls us to be the people of God. We remember that we were created for life with God, who is Father, Son, and Holy Spirit.

One of the prayer services in this section will help students pray for peace in our world. We join our prayers with others as we seek to live as peacemakers. Students can pray the rosary together using the mysteries of light to praise God for all he has done for us in Jesus Christ. Students will be encouraged to help the poor in a prayer service about giving. Another prayer service helps the students thank God for all our gifts and blessings. They can celebrate the example of the saints through prayer services honoring St. Vincent de Paul, St. Thérèse, and celebrating All Saints Day.

Activities in each prayer service involve the students and show them how to follow Jesus Christ in their lives. Students can make peace posters, roses for Jesus, and thank you leaves. A saint prayer table will help students learn about the example of the saints. An idea is also given for encouraging students to help others by providing birthday party items for children at a homeless shelter. Through their prayers and their actions the students learn to give praise to our God.

Live In Peace

Being Peacemakers in Our World

Opening Prayer

· ·

Leader: Lord Jesus, we come before you today and praise your holy name.

All: We give you thanks for all you have done for us.

Leader: We know that you came for all people, all races, all cultures.

All: May we live always in your peace. Amen.

First Reading

· ·

Reader: A reading from the letter of Paul to the Colossians (3:15–17).

The peace that Christ gives is to guide you in the decisions you make; for it is to this peace that God has called you together in one body. And be thankful. Christ's message in all its richness must live in your hearts. Teach and instruct one another with all wisdom. Sing psalms, hymns, and sacred songs; sing to God with thanksgiving in your hearts. Everything you do or say, then, should be done in the name of the Lord Jesus, as you give thanks through him to God the Father.

The word of the Lord.

All: Thanks be to God.

Psalm Prayer (135: 1-3, 13, 19-21)

Leader: Let us now praise God with our psalm recited in two parts.

Left: Praise the Lord! Praise his name, you servants of the Lord, who stand in the Lord's house, in the Temple of our God!

Right: Praise the Lord, because he is good; sing praises to his name, because he is kind.

Left: Lord, you will always be proclaimed as God; all generations will remember you.

Right: Praise the Lord, people of Israel; praise him, you priests of God!

Left: Praise the Lord, you Levites; praise him, all you that worship him!

Right: Praise the Lord in Zion, in Jerusalem, his home. Praise the Lord!

Gospel Reading

Gospel reader:

A reading from the holy gospel according to Matthew (5:23–24).

So if you are about to offer your gift to God at the altar and there you remember that your brother has something against you, leave your gift there in front of the altar, go at once and make peace with your brother, and then come back and offer your gift to God.

The gospel of the Lord.

All: Praise to you, Lord Jesus Christ.

Reflection

Leader: Jesus Christ came for all people, all nations, all races, all cultures. We are called to be peacemakers in our world today. We must also pray for peace. If we have hurt someone by our words or actions, we must ask forgiveness of them. If we are holding grudges, we must forgive in our hearts. We are to live in peace in the name of Jesus Christ.

Peace Posters

Encourage the students to make peace posters before the prayer service. Provide 11″ x 14″ sheets of white poster board and have colorful markers on hand. Students can work in pairs to create posters with drawings and words that promote ways to live in peace. Display the posters in the area where the prayer service will be held.

Intercessions

Leader: We now offer our prayers and our petitions to our Lord Jesus Christ.

Our response to each petition is:
God of peace, hear our prayer.

Reader 1: For victims of violence, may there be an end to the fighting and injustice in our world.

Reader 2: For leaders of nations, may they seek peace with one another for the good of all people.

Reader 3: For those who live with discrimination, may there be an end to the hatred.

Reader 4: For the church throughout the world, may we work for justice and peace.

Reader 5: For all of us gathered here, may we treat people of all races and cultures with respect.

Leader: May we also live in peace in the ways shown on our peace posters. We ask you, Lord Jesus Christ, to hear all our prayers. Amen.

Sign of Peace

Leader: Let us offer one another a sign of God's peace.

All: (To one another) Peace be with you.

(Response) And also with you.

Prayer of St. Francis

Leader: Let us pray the beautiful Peace Prayer of St. Francis.

Left: Lord, make me an instrument of your peace.
Where there is hatred, let me sow love;
where there is injury, pardon;
where there is doubt, faith;
where there is despair, hope;
where there is darkness, light, and
where there is sadness, joy.

Right: O, Divine Master,
grant that I may not so much seek
to be consoled as to console;
to be understood as to understand;
to be loved as to love.
For it is in giving that we receive;
it is in pardoning that we are pardoned;
and it is in dying that we are born to eternal life.

Closing Prayer

Leader: Lord Jesus, you call us to be peacemakers in our world today. Let peace begin with each one of us.

All: Amen.

Works of Mercy

Remembering St. Vincent De Paul

Opening Prayer

Leader: Let us pray. God of all people, we come together today to celebrate the love you have for each of us. We remember that we are to share that love with others.

All: Help us to live in your love.

Leader: You give us the example of St. Vincent de Paul who worked among the poor. He tried to make life better for those in need. May we remember that we too are to serve others in the name of Jesus Christ.

All: Amen.

First Reading

Reader: A reading from the first letter of John (4:7–11).

Dear friends, let us love one another, because love comes from God. Whoever loves is a child of God and knows God. Whoever does not love does not know God, for God is love. And God showed his love by sending his only Son into the world, so that we might have life through him. This is what love is: it is not that we have loved God, but that he loved us and sent his Son to be the means by which our sins are forgiven. Dear friends, if this is how God loved us, then we should love one another.

The word of the Lord.

All: Thanks be to God.

Psalm Prayer (Psalm 146:1-2, 6-7, 10)

Leader: We now lift up our voices in praise to God.

Left: Praise the Lord! Praise the Lord, my soul!
            I will praise him as long as I live;
            I will sing to my God all my life.

Right: He always keeps his promises;
            he judges in favor of the oppressed
            and gives food to the hungry.

Left: The Lord is king forever.

            Your God, O Zion, will reign for all time.

            Praise the Lord!

Gospel Reading

(Before the prayer service, ask for volunteers to read the parts of the narrator, the king, and a person. This dramatic reading brings the gospel alive for students.)

Narrator: A reading from the holy gospel according to Matthew (25:34–40).

            Then the King will say to the people on his right,

King: "Come, you that are blessed by my Father! Come and possess the kingdom which has been prepared for you ever since the creation of the world. I was hungry and you fed me, thirsty and you gave me a drink; I was a stranger and you received me in your homes, naked and you clothed me; I was sick and you took care of me, in prison and you visited me."

Narrator:	The righteous will then answer him,
Person:	"When, Lord, did we ever see you hungry and feed you, or thirsty and give you a drink? When did we ever see you a stranger and welcome you in our homes, or naked and clothe you? When did we ever see you sick or in prison, and visit you?"
Narrator:	The King will reply,
King:	"I tell you, whenever you did for one of these least important of these followers of mine, you did it for me!"
Narrator:	The gospel of the Lord.
All:	Praise to you, Lord Jesus Christ

Reflection

St. Vincent de Paul lived this gospel and saw Jesus Christ in others. St. Vincent lived in France and worked among the poor people in the towns and countryside outside the city of Paris. He brought food and clothing to those in need. He brought medicine to the sick. St. Vincent is an example to all of us of the importance of reaching out to others.

Classroom Collection

Some teachers in schools in low income areas do not have enough classroom supplies. Collect items needed by a teacher to enrich learning for the students in his or her class. In this way students who have more can share with students who have less. Encourage the students to bring in items and send a note home explaining this project. Students bring the items they are donating to the prayer service. Items such as the following are good: flash cards, phonics games, alphabet bingo, books for beginning readers, art supplies, calculators, plastic shoe boxes, dictionaries, chalkboard erasers, overhead markers, copy paper, manila envelopes, pencils, sticky notes, tape, staplers and staples. (You may wish to consult a teacher or principal to see what specific needs their school has.)

Leader: If you have classroom supplies to donate for the class we are helping, please bring them forward at this time. Thank you for sharing with others. (Students bring forward donated items and place them in the collection box.)

Intercessions

Leader: We ask the Lord to hear the prayers we offer today. Our response to each petition is: God of love, hear our prayer.

Reader 1:   May we love one another as Jesus loves us.

All: God of love, hear our prayer.

Reader 2:   May we live as followers of Jesus in all that we do.

All: God of love, hear our prayer.

Reader 3:   May we make the world a better place one day at a time.

All: God of love, hear our prayer.

Reader 4:   May we work for justice for all people in our world.

All: God of love, hear our prayer.

Reader 5:   May we see the face of Jesus in each person we meet.

All: God of love, hear our prayer.

Closing Prayer

Leader: Father of us all, we thank you for the gift of this day and the gift of one another. Help us to remember that all of us are brothers and sisters in Christ. Fill us with your love that we may reach out to others in your name. May we see you in others as did St. Vincent de Paul.

All: Send us your Spirit that we may live in justice and walk in peace each day. Amen.

Honoring St. Thérèse

Opening Prayer

Leader:　We celebrate the life of St. Thérèse who was also known as the Little Flower. St. Thérèse tried to do her best in the small things of everyday life. She was a person of prayer in all that she did. She talked to God in her own words and trusted that God knew what was in her heart.

All:　May we live as Jesus Christ taught us each day. Amen.

First Reading

Reader:　A reading from the first letter of Paul to the Corinthians (13:4–7).

Love is patient and kind; it is not jealous, or conceited or proud; love is not ill-mannered or selfish or irritable; love does not keep a record of wrongs; love is not happy with evil, but is happy with the truth. Love never gives up; and its faith, hope, and patience never fail.

The word of the Lord.

All:　Thanks be to God.

Psalm Prayer (147:1-5, 7-8, 11-12)

Leader:　Let us now praise our God with our psalm recited in two parts.

Left: Praise the Lord!
         It is good to sing praise to our God;
         it is pleasant and right to praise him.

Right: The Lord is restoring Jerusalem;
         he is bringing back the exiles.
         He heals the broken-hearted;
         and bandages their wounds.

Left: He has decided the number of stars
         and calls each one by name.
         Great and mighty is our Lord;
         his wisdom cannot be measured.

Right: Sing hymns of praise to the Lord;
         play music on the harp to our God.

Left: He spreads clouds over the sky;
         he provides rain for the earth
         and makes grass grow on the hills.

Right: He takes pleasure in those who honor him,
         in those who trust in his constant love.
         Praise the Lord, O Jerusalem!

Gospel Reading

Gospel reader:

A reading from the holy gospel according to Mark
(9:33–35).

They came to Capernaum, and after going indoors Jesus
asked his disciples, "What were you arguing about on the
road?" But they would not answer him, because on the
road they had been arguing among themselves about
who was the greatest. Jesus sat down, called the twelve
disciples, and said to them, "Whoever wants to be first
must place himself last of all and be the servant of all."

The gospel of the Lord.

All: Praise to you, Lord Jesus Christ.

A Rose for Jesus

Talk with the students the week before the prayer service about the life of St. Thérèse. Ask them to imitate St. Thérèse by being kind to others without expecting a reward. Hand out Rose for Jesus cards to the students. Ask the students to fill out their cards with a kind act they will do for others and bring the cards to the prayer service. To make the Rose for Jesus cards use half sheets of paper card. The card has a picture of a rose with the title "Rose for Jesus." The card states "I will do good for others like St. Thérèse by". Then there are lines on which each students can write out something they will do for someone else. At the bottom is a line where they sign their name. Duplicate the cards so each student will have one.

Leader: St. Thérèse loved God with all her heart. She tried to be nice to everyone. She promised to spend her time in heaven doing good for people and showering them with roses. As a sign that we will follow the example of St. Thérèse in caring about others, bring forward your Rose for Jesus cards and place them in the basket on the prayer table. (Students place their cards in the basket.)

Intercessions

Leader: Let us now offer our prayers to the God who calls all of us to live a life of love. Our response to each statement is: Lord, help us to be like St. Thérèse.

Reader 1: St. Thérèse prayed to Jesus through everything she did. Even while she was doing chores, she did them for Jesus.

All: Lord, help us to be like St. Thérèse.

Reader 2: St. Thérèse was always kind to others. Even when people criticized her or were ungrateful, she responded with kindness.

All: Lord, help us to be like St. Thérèse.

Reader 3: St. Thérèse turned to Jesus in times of happiness, in times of sadness, and in times of trouble. She was always faithful.

All: Lord, help us to be like St. Thérèse.

Reader 4: St. Thérèse was a holy person who shared her time with others. She was patient with other people and listened to them.

All: Lord, help us to be like St. Thérèse.

Reader 5: St. Thérèse loved everyone, including those who were not nice to her. She said her vocation was love.

All: Lord, help us to be like St. Thérèse.

Closing Prayer

Leader: God of all people, you gave us St. Thérèse as an example of holiness. She was patient and kind to everyone who came her way. Help us to be like St. Thérèse and do the best we can each day. May we share the love of Jesus Christ with others.

All: Amen.

Mysteries of Light

Praying With Our Lady of The Rosary

Praying the Rosary

Before praying the rosary with the students ask for five volunteers. Each one announces one of the five decades and reads the reflection on that mystery. Explain that individual students take turns leading the first half of each prayer of the rosary. All the students respond together with the conclusion of each prayer.

Introduction

Leader: We celebrate Our Lady of the Rosary each year. Through the rosary we give praise to God and ask Mary to pray for us. The rosary helps us remember all that Jesus Christ did for us. Today we will reflect on the mysteries of light as we pray the rosary together. These mysteries celebrate five events in the public life of Jesus Christ. As we pray these mysteries we remember that Jesus Christ is the light of the world and the light we are to follow.

The Five Luminous Mysteries

Reader 1: The First Mystery: The Baptism of Jesus in the Jordan.

Jesus Christ came to John the Baptist at the Jordan River and asked John to baptize him. As Jesus came up out of the water, the Spirit of God came to him. A voice came from above saying "This is my own dear Son, with whom

I am pleased." After his baptism Jesus Christ went forward with his ministry. Each of us is called through our baptism to live as followers of Jesus Christ. We now pray. . . .

Reader 2: The Second Mystery: The Wedding at Cana.

At the wedding feast at Cana, Jesus changed water into wine. This was the first public miracle that he worked and it was at the request of his mother, Mary. The miracles of Jesus Christ are signs of God's glory among us. The miracles reveal to us that Jesus is the Son of God. We too are called to belief in Jesus Christ. We now pray. . . .

Reader 3: The Third Mystery: The Proclamation of the Kingdom.

At the beginning of his ministry in Galilee Jesus proclaimed: The kingdom of God is at hand. Jesus shows us the way to the Father. He reveals the Father to us. We are to be people who help bring about the kingdom of God. We are called to proclaim the good news of Jesus in all we say and do. We now pray. . . .

Reader 4: The Fourth Mystery: The Transfiguration of Jesus Christ.

One day Jesus Christ took three of his disciples up on a high mountain. There he was transfigured before them and his clothes became white as light. The apostles heard a voice proclaim "This is my own dear Son with whom I am pleased—listen to him!" The glory of God shined through Jesus. We too need to go up to the mountain and reflect on the glory of God and then go down the mountain to live out our faith in Jesus Christ. We now pray. . . .

Reader 5: The Fifth Mystery: The Eucharist.

At the Last Supper Jesus Christ offered himself to his disciples in the bread and in the wine. At Mass we remember that Jesus gives himself to us in the eucharist out of love. In this way he is with us always and we share in his life. As people of the Eucharist, we are united in Jesus. We are called to serve others in his name. We now pray. . . .

Closing

. . . .

Leader: We have now prayed five decades of the rosary and reflected on the mysteries of light. We remember all that Jesus Christ did for us. We ask Mary to pray for us that we may be faithful to God as she was. Let us give glory to God in all that we do.

All: Thanks be to God.

Give to Others

Helping the Poor

Opening Prayer

Leader: Father of us all, we come together to give glory to your holy name. We ask that you open our hearts to the needs of others. All around us there are people struggling with poverty, with illness, and with problems of every kind. Help us to remember that we are called to give of ourselves and of what we have to others. May we reach out to those in need. In this way we become like Jesus Christ, who cared about all people.

All: Help us, Jesus, to walk in your way of love. Amen.

First Reading

Reader: A reading from the letter of James (2:14–17).

My friends, what good is it for one of you to say that you have faith if your actions do not prove it? Can that faith save you? Suppose there are brothers or sisters who need clothes and don't have enough to eat. What good is there in your saying to them, "God bless you! Keep warm and eat well!"—if you don't give them the necessities of life? So it is with faith: if it is alone and includes no actions, then it is dead.

The word of the Lord.

All: Thanks be to God.

Psalm Prayer (150:1-2, 6)

Leader: Let us give praise to the Lord by praying our psalm together.

All: Praise the Lord!
Praise God in his Temple!
Praise his strength in heaven!
Praise him for the mighty things he has done.
Praise his supreme greatness.
Praise the Lord, all living creatures!
Praise the Lord!

Gospel Reading

(Before the prayer service, ask for volunteers to read the parts of the narrator, the rich man and Jesus. This dramatic reading brings the gospel alive for students.)

Narrator: A reading from the holy gospel according to Matthew (19:16–22).

Once a man came to Jesus and asked,

Rich man: "Teacher, what good thing must I do to receive eternal life?"

Narrator: Jesus answered,

Jesus: "Why do you ask me concerning what is good? There is only One who is good. Keep the commandments if you want to enter into life."

Narrator: The man asked,

Rich man: "What commandments?"

Narrator: Jesus answered,

Jesus: "Do not commit murder; do not commit adultery; do not steal; do not accuse anyone falsely; respect your father and your mother; and love your neighbor as you love yourself."

Narrator: The young man replied,

Rich man: "I have obeyed all these commandments. What else do I need to do?"

Narrator: Jesus said to him,

Jesus: "If you want to be perfect, go and sell all you have and give the money to the poor, and you will have riches in heaven; then come and follow me."

Narrator: When the young man heard this, he went away sad, because he was very rich.

The gospel of the Lord.

All: Praise to you, Lord, Jesus Christ.

Birthday Party Project

The week before the prayer service explain to the students that families who live in homeless shelters do not have the means to provide a birthday party for their children. The students can bring in items for the shelter that can be used for children's birthday parties. Send home a note to the parents about this project. Provide a box in which the students can place their contributions as part of the prayer service. A birthday party collection enables children to reach out to other children. Birthday items needed include: cake mixes, tubs of frosting, candles, cups and plates, tablecloths, cards, wrapping paper, and gifts such as toys and games. (You may want to arrange for this donation with the Volunteer Coordinator prior to the service.)

Leader: Let us now bring forward the birthday party items we have brought for the children who live in shelters. Place your item in the birthday box. Thank you for opening your hearts to children in need. (Students bring birthday party supplies forward.)

Intercessions

· ·

Leader: We pray for the needs of children around the world. Our response is: Lord, hear our prayer.

Reader 1:   For the children in India who cried this morning because there was no food for them to eat, we pray to the Lord.

All: Lord, hear our prayer.

Reader 2:   For children in Somalia who had to leave everything behind to flee from war, we pray to the Lord.

All: Lord, hear our prayer.

Reader 3:   For children in Russia who do not have warm winter jackets to wear to school and whose hands are cold without gloves, we pray to the Lord.

All: Lord, hear our prayer.

Reader 4:   For children in Guatemala who are seriously ill and don't have access to the medical care they need, we pray to the Lord.

All: Lord, hear our prayer.

Reader 5:   For children in the United States who are homeless and who live in shelters, we pray to the Lord.

All: Lord, hear our prayer.

Leader: Lord Jesus Christ, we offer our prayers for all your children. Amen.

Closing Prayer

· ·

Leader: Loving Father and Creator of all people, we ask your blessing on us and on the children of the world. May we see the needs of others and share what we have been given. Help us to be people of compassion and mercy.

All: We ask this through our Lord, Jesus Christ, and your Holy Spirit of love. Amen.

honor the Saints

Celebrating All Saints Day

Saint Table

Set up a saint table in the area where the prayer service will be held. Cover a small table with a cloth. Add a gold cross in the center. Frame saint pictures from note cards and set them on the table on either side of the cross. This parade of saints will remind the students of the many people who have followed God's will in their lives. Leave up the saint table throughout the month of November.

Opening Prayer

· ·

Leader: We gather together to remember the saints as we prepare to celebrate All Saints Day. The lives of the saints give glory to God. They are examples for all of us.

All: Father of love and mercy, help us to give glory and praise to your name as do your holy saints.

Leader: The saints followed the word of God in all they did. They lived the commandment of Jesus to love God and love others. All of us are called to be saints.

All: Lord Jesus Christ, you are the teacher of all of us. May we follow your way of love always.

Leader: As we celebrate the lives of the saints, we remember that the road will not always be easy. We should always do what is right and pleasing to God. May we become all that God created us to be.

All: Holy Spirit of love, be with us and guide us in all that we do. Amen.

First Reading

· ·

Reader: A reading from the book of Isaiah (61:1–2).

The Sovereign Lord has filled me with his Spirit. He has chosen me and sent me to bring good news to the poor, to heal the broken-hearted, to announce release to captives and freedom to those in prison. He has sent me to proclaim that the time has come when the Lord will save his people and defeat their enemies. He has sent me to comfort all who mourn.

The word of the Lord.

All: Thanks be to God.

Psalm Prayer (136:1-9)

Leader: We now give praise to God with our psalm prayer.

Left: Give thanks to the Lord, because he is good;
his love is eternal.
Give thanks to the greatest of all gods;
his love is eternal.

Right: Give thanks to the mightiest of all lords;
his love is eternal.
He alone performs great miracles;
his love is eternal.

Left: By his wisdom he made the heavens;
his love is eternal;
he built the earth on the deep waters;
his love is eternal.

Right: He made the sun and the moon;
his love is eternal;
the sun to rule over the day;
his love is eternal;
the moon and the stars to rule over the night;
his love is eternal.

Gospel Reading

Gospel reader:

A reading from the holy gospel according to John
(14:18–21).

When I go, you will not be left all alone; I will come
back to you. In a little while the world will see me no
more, but you will see me; and because I live, you also
will live. When that day comes, you will know that I am
in my Father and that you are in me, just as I am in you.
Those who accept my commandments and obey them

are the ones who love me. My Father will love those who love me; I too will love them and reveal myself to them.

The gospel of the Lord.

All: Praise to you, Lord Jesus Christ.

Reflection

As we celebrate All Saints Day, we remember that God calls each of us to be saints. God created each of us for life with the Trinity. We are to live in holiness each day. Think about these questions. How is God calling me? How can I serve God now and in the future? What can I do to give praise to God? How does God want me to reach out to others? What God-given talents and abilities can I use for the glory of God?

Saint Litany

Leader: We ask the saints in heaven to pray to God for us and for all people. Our response is: Pray for us.

Litany reader:

        Holy Mary, queen of heaven and earth . . . Pray for us.
        St. Joseph, person who did God's will . . . Pray for us.
        St. Matthew, apostle of Jesus Christ . . . Pray for us.
        St. Elizabeth, cousin of Mary . . . Pray for us.
        St. Thomas, person of faith and love . . . Pray for us.
        St. John, beloved disciple of Jesus Christ . . . Pray for us.
        St. Monica, person of prayer and hope . . . Pray for us.
        St. Juan Diego, faithful follower . . . Pray for us.
        All the saints of God's kingdom . . . Pray for us.

Leader: Let us now pray together the prayer that Jesus taught us.

All: Our Father. . . .

Closing Prayer

Leader: God calls us to live in faithfulness. We are to follow God's way of love at all times and in all places. All of us are called to be saints in the kingdom of God.

All: May our lives give glory to God in all that we say and all that we do.

Closing Blessing

Leader: May God bless our lives today and always. In the name of the Father, and of the Son, and of the Holy Spirit.

All: Amen.

Give Thanks to God

Praising Our Creator at Thanksgiving

Opening Prayer

Leader: God, we come before you today as your people. We honor you as the Creator of our universe and everything in it.

All: We give glory to your holy name.

Leader: God, help us to remember that all that we have and all that we are come from you. You have made a beautiful world for us.

All: We give you thanks for everything you have made.

Leader: God, everything you have given us is good. May we be wise stewards of all you have created, sharing the resources of our world with others.

All: We give you praise for all of creation. Amen.

First Reading

Reader: A reading from the book of Genesis (1:3–5).

Then God commanded, "Let there be light"—and light appeared. God was pleased with what he saw. Then he separated the light from the darkness, and he named the light "Day" and the darkness "Night."

The word of the Lord.

All: Thanks be to God.

Psalm Prayer (95:1-6)

Leader: Let us pray our psalm prayer in parts.

Left: Come, let us praise the Lord!
            Let us sing for joy to God, who protects us!

Right: Let us come before him with thanksgiving
            and sing joyful songs of praise.

Left: For the Lord is a mighty God,
            a mighty king over all the gods.

Right: He rules over the whole earth,
            from the deepest caves to the highest hills.

Left: He rules over the sea, which he made;
            the land also, which he himself formed.

Right: Come, let us bow down and worship him;
            let us kneel before the Lord, our Maker!

Gospel Reading

Gospel reader:

A reading from the holy gospel according to John (1:1–4).

In the beginning the Word already existed; the Word was
with God, and the Word was God. From the very
beginning the Word was with God. Through him God
made all things; not one thing in all creation was made
without him. The Word was the source of life, and this
life brought light to people.

The gospel of the Lord.

All: Praise to you, Lord Jesus Christ.

Thank You Leaves

- -

Duplicate the thank you leaves on fall colors of copy paper such as gold, orange, red, and green. Four leaves fit on each page. Cut apart in squares. Have several leaves available for each student and ask them to write down something on each leaf for which they are thankful to God. In this way they learn to give thanks to God for the world and the people around them. Have the students bring their leaves as they gather together for prayer.

Leader: There are many things for which we can be thankful to our God. Each of you is now invited to come forward and place your thank you leaves in the basket on our prayer table.

Litany

Leader: We give thanks to God who is the Creator of our world. Our response is: Thank you, God.

Reader 1:   For the sun that shines in the daytime, for the stars that glow at night, for the moon that lights up the dark night,

All: Thank you, God.

Reader 2:   For flowers of every color, for trees of every size, for plants that give us food to eat, for trees that grow ever upward,

All: Thank you, God.

Reader 3:   For all the animals that roam the jungles and forests, for the fish that swim in the sea, for the birds that fly in the sky,

All: Thank you, God.

Reader 4:   For the high mountain tops and the deep oceans, for lakes and clear streams, for the rain that helps everything grow,

All: Thank you, God.

Reader 5:   For people of all nations and races, for people of all abilities and ages, for all the people you have created,

All: Thank you, God.

Reader 6:   For all the things you have made that we have written on our thank you leaves,

All: Thank you, God.

Closing Prayer

● ●

Leader: God, we give you thanks for all the blessings you have given us. May we always remember your unending love for each of us. Help us to see the beauty of our world and the hope that each day brings. Open our hearts to the love in our lives and the people who care for us.

All: Teach us to use the gifts we have been given for the glory of your name. Amen.

Winter

The winter section features prayer services that can be used in the classroom during the winter months of December, January, and February. The prayer services help students celebrate the church year and their lives as the people of God. These prayer services reflect the hope that the coming of Jesus Christ brings to our lives.

The wonderful season of Advent should be a prayerful time for all of us. It is a season of hope and a season of waiting. During the Christmas season we celebrate together the great miracle of the birth of Jesus Christ in a stable. We must help the students make the connection between the Christ Child of Christmas and the risen Christ of Easter. At the conclusion of the Christmas season the church moves into the first weeks of Ordinary Time. This is when we learn how to follow Jesus Christ in our lives each day.

Prayer services are included for Advent to celebrate the hope of this season and all it can be. A Christmas prayer service helps the students give glory to God for the coming of Jesus Christ. We celebrate that Jesus came for all people and all nations through the story of the wise men. As we move into the season of Ordinary Time we pray that we may have faith in God in all things. We are encouraged to follow the example of St. Peter who was a person of great faith.

Activities in each prayer service will help the students pray together and live the gospels. Students will be given Advent prayer cards to encourage them to pray at home also during this season. They will learn to reach out to children in need and give the gift of their concern at Christmas. The students will proclaim in parts the story of the faith of the blind man and draw listeners into this story that speaks to all of us.

Light of the World

Lighting the Advent Wreath

Opening Prayer

Leader: Jesus, you are the light of the world.

All: Guide us to live in your light.

Leader: Jesus, you are the light that shines in the darkness.

All: May we turn from selfishness toward your light.

Leader: Jesus, you are the light for all nations.

All: Help us to follow you always. Amen.

Lighting the Advent Wreath

(A simple way to make an Advent wreath is with a plain 18″ evergreen door wreath. Lay it flat and place three purple candles and one pink candle around the wreath. Three-inch-wide pillar candles work great. This type of Advent wreath is large enough for all the students to see and lasts year after year. Light the candle during the prayer service.)

Leader: Lord, during this holy season of Advent we wait in hope for your coming. Today, as we gather around our Advent wreath, we light a candle for each of the four weeks of the Advent season. As the light grows brighter, we will know that Christmas is closer. May the candles of this wreath remind us that you are the light of the world.

All: Help us to live in the light of your love each day of our lives. Amen.

First Reading

Reader: A reading from Book of Isaiah (9:2–3, 6).

The people who walked in darkness have seen a great light. They lived in a land of shadows, but now light is shining on them. You have given them great joy, Lord; you have made them happy. They rejoice in what you have done. . . . A child is born to us! A son is given to us! And he will be our ruler.

The word of the Lord.

All: Thanks be to God

Psalm Prayer: (113:1-4)

Leader: We now praise God with our psalm prayer.

Left: Praise the Lord!
You servants of the Lord,
praise his name!

Right: May his name be praised,
now and forever.

Left: From the east to the west
praise the name of the Lord!

Right: The Lord rules over all nations;
his glory is above the heavens.

Gospel Reading

Gospel reader:

Let us listen to the Word of God that speaks to our minds and hearts as Christians. Today's reading is just one verse, so pay close attention! A reading from the holy gospel according to John (8:12).

Jesus spoke to the Pharisees again. "I am the light of the world," he said. "Whoever follows me will have the light of life and will never walk in darkness."

The gospel of the Lord.

All: Praise to you, Lord Jesus Christ.

Reflection Prayer

Leader: We have heard God's word, now let us reflect on how we are called to live in the light of Christ. Our response is: Lord, help us to walk in your light.

Reader 1: We live in darkness when we are cruel to another person.

We live in the light of Christ when we are people of compassion.

All: Lord, help us to walk in your light.

Reader 2: We walk in darkness when we use words to hurt someone.

We live as people in the light of Christ when we give encouragement to others.

All: Lord, help us to walk in your light.

Reader 3: We live in darkness when we are selfish.

We live in the light of Christ when we give food to the poor and comfort to the sick

All: Lord, help us to walk in your light.

Reader 4: We live in darkness when we do not stand up for the rights of others.

We walk in the light of Christ when we work for justice in our world.

All: Lord, help us to walk in your light.

Reader 5: We live in darkness when we have hate in our hearts.

We live in the light of Christ when we care about other people.

All: Lord, help us to walk in your light.

Closing Prayer

Leader: Christ, be our light in all that we do during this holy season of Advent and beyond. Open our minds and our hearts to your ways of love. Help us to remember that you came for all nations and all people. May the light of your love shine through us so that others will come to know you.

All: Help us to walk always in your light. Amen.

Closing Blessing

Leader: We ask God's blessing on us all in the name of the Father, and of the Son, and of the Holy Spirit.

All: Amen.

Live in hope

Helping Others During Advent

Opening Prayer

Leader: Advent is a time to prepare ourselves for the coming of Jesus Christ in all that we say and do.

All: We wait in joyful hope.

Leader: Advent is a time to reach out to others in the spirit of love and share what we have been given.

All: We wait in joyful hope.

Leader: Advent is a time to remember all that God has done for us and give praise to God's name.

All: We wait in joyful hope.

First Reading

Reader: A reading from the prophet Isaiah (40:3–5).

A voice cries out, "Prepare in the wilderness a road for the Lord! Clear the way in the desert for our God! Fill every valley; level every mountain. The hills will become a plain, and the rough country will be made smooth. Then the glory of the Lord will be revealed, and all people will see it. The Lord himself has promised this."

The word of the Lord.

All: Thanks be to God.

Psalm Prayer (33:1-5, 20-22)

Leader: We offer praise to our God with our psalm prayer.

Left: Shout for joy for what the Lord has done;
            praise him, all you that obey him.
            Give thanks to the Lord with harps,
            sing to him with stringed instruments.

Right: Sing a new song to him,
            play the harp with skill, and shout for joy!
            The words of the Lord are true,
            all his works are dependable.

Left: The Lord loves what is righteous and just;
            his constant love fills the earth.
            We put our hope in the Lord;
            he is our protector and our help.

Right: We are glad because of him;
            we trust in his holy name.
            May your constant love be with us, Lord,
            as we put our hope in you.

Gospel Reading

Gospel reader:

            A reading from the holy gospel according to Mark
            (10:42–45).

            So Jesus called them all together to him and said . . . "If
            one of you wants to be great, you must be the servant of
            the rest; and if one of you want to be first, you must be
            the slave of all. For even the Son of Man did not come to
            be served; he came to serve and to give his life to
            redeem many people."

            The holy gospel of the Lord.

All: Praise to you, Lord Jesus Christ.

Children's Center Collection

To help the students live this gospel, ask them to bring in items for a local organization that serves children in crisis. Explain the need for this project and send a letter home to parents asking for their help. Give them a list of items needed by the center such as books, sweatshirts, hats, puzzles, art supplies, footballs, basketballs, movie passes, discount store certificates, coloring books and crayons. (Prior to the service, consult with the coordinator of a local agency to determine their specific needs.) Place a marked box for the collection in the area where the prayer service will be held.

Leader: You may now bring forward any items you have brought for the crisis center. Thank you for sharing with others during this season of Advent. (Students place donated items in the collection box.)

Intercessions

Leader: We offer our Advent prayers to the Lord who knows our hearts.

Reader 1: May we live in love during this holy season and always, we pray to the Lord.

All: God of love, hear our prayer.

Reader: 2: May we live in justice and treat all people with respect, we pray to the Lord.

All: God of justice, hear our prayer.

Reader 3: May we live in joy and proclaim the good news to all people, we pray to the Lord.

All: God of joy, hear our prayer.

Reader 4:   May we live in peace in our families, our community,
            and our world, we pray to the Lord.

All: God of peace, hear our prayer.

Reader 5:   May we live in hope and know that God is always with
            us, we pray to the Lord.

All: God of hope, hear our prayer.

Closing Prayer

Leader: May we walk in God's love in all that we do during
            Advent and always. As we prepare to celebrate the
            coming of Jesus Christ among us, let us open our hearts
            to the needs of others.

All: Lord, help us to follow your way of love in our lives.
            Amen.

Waiting for Jesus

Praising God in the Advent Season

Opening Prayer

Leader: We come together today during this holy Advent season to give praise to God. We prepare to celebrate the coming of Jesus into our hearts and our lives. God loves us with an unending love. We are called to share the love of God with others.

All: Lord God, you are the source of all love and all that is good. May we learn to love others in your name. Amen.

First Reading

Reader: A reading from the book of Jeremiah (33:14–15).

The Lord said,

"The time is coming when I will fulfill the promise that I made to the people of Israel and Judah. At that time I will choose as king a righteous descendant of David. That king will do what is right and just throughout the land."

The word of the Lord.

All: Thanks be to God.

Psalm Prayer (89:1-2)

Leader: We praise God together with our psalm prayer.

All: O Lord, I will always sing of your constant love;
            I will proclaim your faithfulness forever.
            I know that your love will last for all time,
            that your faithfulness is as permanent as the sky.

Gospel Reading

Gospel reader:

A reading from the holy gospel according to Mark (1:4–5, 7–9).

So John appeared in the desert, baptizing and preaching. "Turn away from your sins and be baptized," he told the people, "and God will forgive your sins." Many people from the province of Judea and the city of Jerusalem went out to hear John. . . He announced to the people, "The man who will come after me is much greater than I am. I am not good enough even to bend down and untie his sandals. I baptize you with water, but he will baptize you with the Holy Spirit."

The gospel of the Lord.

All: Praise to you, Lord Jesus Christ.

Intercessions

Leader: We now bring our petitions before the God of all of us. Our response is: Lord, teach us to love.

Reader 1:   May we love one another as God loves us: with an unending love.

All: Lord, teach us to love.

Reader 2:   May we give to those in need in our world, especially the homeless.

All: Lord, teach us to love.

Reader 3:   May we ask forgiveness of those we have hurt by our actions and words.

All: Lord, teach us to love.

Reader 4:   May we grant forgiveness to those who have hurt us.

All: Lord, teach us to love.

Reader 5:   May we work for justice for all people, even when it is difficult.

All: Lord, teach us to love.

Reader 6:   May we see the face of Jesus Christ in everyone we meet.

All: Lord, teach us to love.

Leader: Lord, we ask you to hear these prayers and all the prayers that are in our hearts. Amen.

Advent Prayer Card

Make Advent prayer cards for the students. They can use the prayer cards in the prayer service and then at home during the Advent season. Duplicate the closing prayer from the prayer service. Add the words "Advent Prayer" at the top and a picture of an Advent wreath at the bottom. Four copies will fit on one page of blue card stock. Cut apart the prayers to make prayer cards and place them in a basket.

Leader: Come forward now to get an Advent Prayer Card. We will pray this together as our closing prayer, and you can use this prayer at home with your family.

Advent Prayer

Father,
as we wait together in hope during Advent season
we remember all that you have done for us.
We thank you for the gift of your Son, Jesus Christ,
who is the true light of the world.
May we live in love during Advent and always
because of the coming of Jesus Christ.
Help us to share with others, and
treat all people with justice in your name.
All honor and praise be yours forever and ever.
Amen.

Advent Prayer

All: Father, as we wait together in hope
        during this Advent season
        we remember all that you have done for us.
        We thank you for the gift of your Son, Jesus Christ,
        who is the true light of the world.
        May we live in love during Advent and always
        because of the coming of Jesus Christ.
        Help us to share with others,
        and treat all people with justice in your name.
        All honor and praise be yours forever and ever.
        Amen.

Glory to God

Celebrating the Christmas Season

Prayer of Praise

Leader: Glory to God in the highest

All: And peace to God's people on earth.

Leader: Lord God, heavenly King, almighty God and Father

All: We worship you, we give you thanks, we praise you for your glory.

Opening Prayer

Leader: Father of all people, at Christmas we remember all that you have done for us. You sent Jesus Christ to us out of love. Jesus is the best Christmas gift of all. Jesus brought a message of peace and love to the world at Christmas. May his coming help us to open our hearts and lives to the needs of others.

All: May we share the joy of the Christmas season with others in your name. Amen.

First Reading

Reader: A reading from the book of Isaiah (11:1–2).

The royal line of David is like a tree that has been cut down; but just as new branches sprout from a stump, so

a new king will arise from among David's descendants.
The spirit of the Lord will give him wisdom and the
knowledge and skill to rule his people. He will know the
Lord's will and honor him.

The word of the Lord.

All: Thanks be to God.

Psalm Prayer (145:1-10)

Psalm reader 1:

I will proclaim your greatness, my God and king;
I will thank you forever and ever.
Every day I will thank you;
I will praise you forever and ever.

All: Every day I will thank you;
I will praise you forever and ever.

Psalm reader 2:

The Lord is great and is to be highly praised;
his greatness is beyond understanding.
What you have done will be praised
from one generation to the next;
they will proclaim your mighty acts.

All: Every day I will thank you;
I will praise you forever and ever.

Psalm reader 3:

They will speak of your glory and majesty,
and I will meditate on your wonderful deeds.
People will speak of your mighty deeds,
and I will proclaim your greatness.

All: Every day I will thank you;
I will praise you forever and ever.

Psalm reader 4:

>They will tell about all your goodness
>and sing about your kindness.
>The Lord is loving and merciful
>slow to become angry and full of constant love.

All: Every day I will thank you;
              I will praise you forever and ever.

Psalm reader 5:

>The Lord is good to everyone
>and has compassion on all he made.,
>All your creatures, Lord, will praise you,
>and all your people will give you thanks.

All: Every day I will thank you;
              I will praise you forever and ever.

Gospel Reading

(Before the prayer service, ask for volunteers to read the parts of the narrator, an angel, and a shepherd. This dramatic reading brings the gospel alive for students.)

Narrator: This is the story of the first Christmas from the gospel of Luke (2:8–16).

There were some shepherds in that part of the country who were spending the night in the fields, taking care of their flocks. An angel of the Lord appeared to them, and the glory of the Lord shone over them. They were terribly afraid, but the angel said to them,

Angel: "Don't be afraid! I am here with good news for you, which will bring great joy to all the people. This very day in David's town your Savior was born—Christ the Lord! And this is what will prove it to you: you will find a baby wrapped in cloths and lying in a manger."

Narrator: Suddenly a great army of heaven's angels appeared with the angel, singing praises to God:

Angel:	"Glory to God in the highest heaven, and peace on earth to those with whom he is pleased!"
Narrator:	When the angels went away from them back into heaven, the shepherds said to one another,
Shepherd:	"Let's go to Bethlehem and see this thing that has happened, which the Lord has told us."
Narrator:	So they hurried off and found Mary and Joseph and saw the baby lying in the manger.
	The gospel of the Lord.
All:	Praise to you, Lord Jesus Christ.

Christmas Gifts For Jesus

Before class make a form titled "My gift for Jesus at Christmas" on a half sheet of paper. Provide lines to write on and a place for the student to sign their name. Duplicate on green copy paper. During class time talk about giving gifts. Help students think about a gift they can give to Jesus at Christmas. Give them examples such as helping an elderly neighbor, giving a toy to a child in need, or being nice to someone they do not like. Then ask each student to fill out a form and describe the gift they will give to Jesus from their hearts. They bring the completed forms to the prayer service.

My gift for Jesus at Christmas

_____

_____

_____

Signed _____

Leader: We now bring forward our Christmas gifts for the Christ Child and place them in the basket by the manger scene.

(Allow time for students to bring up their Christmas gift forms.)

All: Lord Jesus, we offer you these gifts from our hearts. May we show our love for you by the way we treat others in your name. In this way we live the miracle that is Christmas. Amen.

Intercessions

Leader: We now offer our prayers and petitions to our Lord Jesus Christ. Our response is: Be with us, Lord Jesus.

Reader 1: Mary waited for Jesus as did the world. May we learn to be patient with one another.

All: Be with us, Lord Jesus.

Reader 2: Joseph did his best for Mary and the child, Jesus. May we be faithful to God's will in our lives.

Reader 3: The innkeeper found a place for Mary and Joseph in the stable. May we always have room in our hearts for Jesus.

Reader 4: The angels sang praise to God. May our lives give glory to God in all that we do.

Reader 5: The shepherds went to see the savior who had been born. May we remember that Jesus came for all people.

Closing Prayer

Leader: God, Father of us all, our hearts and our lives are filled with your love. Help us to reach out to those who are sad, alone, or hurting. May we live the season of Christmas all through the year.

All: Amen.

Journey of the Wise Men

Following the Star

Opening Prayer

Leader: We gather together today to celebrate Epiphany. We remember how the wise men came from the East and followed the star. They journeyed on until they came to the place where the child Jesus was.

All: Come, let us adore him.

Leader: The wise men came to give honor to Jesus Christ. Jesus came for all people and all nations.

All: Come, let us adore him.

Leader: We too are to follow the star of Jesus Christ in our lives. We are to go where God leads us.

All: Come, let us adore him.

Wise Men Procession

Before the prayer service, ask for three volunteers to represent the wise men. Provide a gold paper crown for each of these students to wear. Also give each student a figure of one of the wise men to place in the class nativity scene.

Leader: To help us remember the journey of the wise men, three students will now come forward to place figures of the wise men in our nativity scene. The wise men came bearing gifts for the Christ Child. We too are to bring him gifts from our hearts and our lives.

All: Help us, Lord, on our faith journey. Amen.

First Reading

Reader: A reading from the book of Isaiah (60:1–3).

Arise, Jerusalem, and shine like the sun; the glory of the Lord is shining on you! Other nations will be covered by darkness, but on you the light of the Lord will shine; the brightness of his presence will be with you. Nations will be drawn to your light, and kings to the dawning of your new day.

The word of the Lord.

All: Thanks be to God.

Psalm Prayer (148:1, 3-6, 9-13)

Leader: Let us recite our psalm prayer in two parts.

Left: Praise the Lord!
Praise the Lord from heaven,
you that live in the heights above.

Right: Praise him, sun and moon;
praise him, shining stars.
Praise him, highest heavens.

Left: Let them all praise the name of the Lord!
He commanded, and they were created;
by his command they were fixed in their places forever.

Right: Praise him, hills and mountains,
fruit trees and forests;
all animals, tame and wild,
reptiles and birds.

Left: Praise him, kings and all peoples,
         princes and all other rules;
         young women and young men,
         old people and children too.

Right: Let them all praise the name of the Lord!
         His name is greater than all others;
         his glory is above earth and heaven.

Gospel Reading

Gospel reader:

A reading about Epiphany from the gospel of Matthew (2:1, 9–11).

Jesus was born in the town of Bethlehem in Judea, during the time when Herod was king. Soon afterward, some men who studied the stars came from the East…and on their way they saw the same star they had seen in the East. When they saw it, how happy they were, what joy was theirs! It went ahead of them until it stopped over the place where the child was. They went into the house, and when they saw the child with his mother Mary, they knelt down and worshiped him. They brought out their gifts of gold, frankincense, and myrrh and presented them to him.

The gospel of the Lord.

All: Praise to you, Lord Jesus Christ.

Intercessions

Leader: We now offer our prayers and petitions to our God. Our response to each petition is: Lord, hear our prayer.

Reader 1: Jesus, we give you the gift of our love. Help us to share love with others, especially the poor.

All: Lord, hear our prayer.

Reader 2: Jesus, we give you the gift of our prayers. Help us to remember to pray for the needs of other people.

All: Lord, hear our prayer.

Reader 3: Jesus, we give you the gift of our faith. Help us to tell others the good news about you.

All: Lord, hear our prayer.

Reader 4: Jesus, we give you the gift of our hearts. Help us to reach out to other people in your name.

All: Lord, hear our prayer.

Reader 5: Jesus, we give you the gift of our lives. Help us to follow your way in all that we do each day.

All: Lord, hear our prayer.

Closing Prayer

Leader: God our Father, we thank you for your unending love for each of us. We give glory to your name for the coming of Jesus Christ at Christmas. We pray that we will live the spirit of the Christmas season all through the year.

All: Help us follow the star of Jesus Christ in our own lives. Amen.

Believe in Jesus Christ

Seeing God in Our Lives

Prayer of Praise

Leader: The Lord be with you.

All: And also with you.

Leader: We gather together to give praise to God.

All: Holy is God's name.

Opening Prayer

Leader: Lord, we come before you today and ask you to heal our hearts and our unfaithfulness. Help us to know your presence in our lives and to live in faith. May we share that faith with others and tell them the good news of Jesus Christ.

All: Amen.

First Reading

Reader: A reading from the book of Isaiah (43:1, 5–7).

Israel, the Lord who created you says, "Do not be afraid—I will save you. I have called you by name—you are mine. . . . From the distant east and the farthest west I will bring your people home. I will tell the north to let them go and the south not to hold them back. Let my people return from distant lands, from every part of the world. They are my own people, and I created them to bring me glory."

The word of the Lord.

All: Thanks be to God.

Psalm Prayer (31:1, 3, 5)

Leader: Let us pray our psalm prayer together:

All: I come to you, Lord, for protection;
          never let me be defeated.
          You are my refuge and defense;
          guide me and lead me as you have promised.
          I place myself in your care.
          You will save me, Lord;
          you are a faithful God.

Gospel Reading

(Before the prayer service, ask for volunteers to read the parts of the narrator, the blind man, and Jesus. This dramatic reading brings the gospel alive for students.)

Narrator: A reading from the holy gospel according to Luke (18:35–43).

            As Jesus was coming near Jericho, there was a blind man sitting by the road, begging. When he heard the crowd passing by, he asked,

Blind man: "What is this?"

Narrator: They told him that Jesus of Nazareth was passing by. He cried out,

Blind man: "Jesus! Son of David! Have mercy on me!"

Narrator: The people in front scolded him and told him to be quiet. But he shouted even more loudly,

Blind man: "Son of David! Have mercy on me!"

Narrator: So Jesus stopped and ordered the blind man to be brought to him. When he came near, Jesus asked him,

Jesus: "What do you want me to do for you?"

Blind man: "Sir, I want to see again."

Narrator: Jesus said to him,

Jesus: "Then see! Your faith has made you well."

Narrator: At once he was able to see, and he followed Jesus, giving thanks to God. When the crowd saw it, they all praised God.

The gospel of the Lord.

All: Praise to you, Lord Jesus Christ.

Reflection

· ·

The blind man in this gospel story is an example for all of us. The blind man knew that Jesus could heal him. Although he was blind, he could see that Jesus was the Messiah. He had faith in Jesus Christ. The other people, who were not blind, could not see who Jesus really was. They did not have faith. We are called to have faith like the blind man. After the man was healed, he got up and followed Jesus Christ. We too should follow Jesus Christ in all that we do.

Intercessions

· ·

Leader: We come before the Lord with our prayers.

Our response is:

Lord, help us to have faith.

Reader 1: May we witness to the presence of Jesus Christ in our lives by all we do.

All: Lord, help us to have faith.

Reader 2: May we not become discouraged when times are tough and things go wrong.

All: Lord, help us to have faith.

Reader 3: May we know what is right and true and follow Jesus Christ always.

All: Lord, help us to have faith.

Reader 4: May we live our faith and open our hearts to people in need in our world.

All: Lord, help us to have faith.

Reader 5: May we help the sick and infirm and bring them the comfort of our care.

All: Lord, help us to have faith.

Reader 6: May we give praise to God by the way live each day of our lives.

All: Lord, help us to have faith.

Leader: Hear our petitions, O Lord. Amen.

Our Father

Leader: Let us pray together the prayer that Jesus taught us.

All: Our Father . . .

Closing Prayer

Leader: Jesus, you cured the blind and the sick and showed that you are Lord of all. We give you praise as the Messiah and Redeemer. You showed us the power of God's love in our world. Help us to follow you always.

All: Lord, help us to live our faith in you each day. Amen.

You Are the Messiah

Honoring St. Peter

Opening Prayer

Leader: Today we honor St. Peter, who was an apostle and a person of great faith. After the resurrection of Jesus Christ and the coming of the Holy Spirit, St. Peter preached the good news far and wide. He witnessed to what Jesus Christ said and did. He was the leader of the early church. We too are called to be faithful followers of Christ in all things.

All: Lord, help us recognize who you are in our lives and to follow you always. Amen.

First Reading

Reader: A reading from the book of Isaiah (43:10–11).

People of Israel, you are my witnesses; I chose you to be my servant, so that you would know me and believe in me and understand that I am the only God. Besides me there is no other god; there never was and never will be. I alone am the Lord.

The word of the Lord.

All: Thanks be to God.

Psalm Prayer (71:1-2)

Leader: Let us pray together our psalm.

All: Lord, I have come to you for protection;
             never let me be defeated!
             Because you are righteous, help me and rescue me.
             Listen to me and save me!

Gospel Reading

(Before the prayer service, ask for volunteers to read the parts of the narrator, Jesus, a disciple, and Peter. This dramatic reading brings the gospel alive for students.)

Narrator: A reading from the holy gospel according to Matthew (16:13–18).

             Jesus went to the territory near the town of Caesarea Philippi, where he asked his disciples,

Jesus: "Who do people say the Son of Man is?"

Narrator: They answered,

Disciple: "Some say John the Baptist. Others say Elijah, while others say Jeremiah or some other prophet."

Jesus: "What about you? Who do you say I am?"

Narrator: Simon Peter answered,

Peter: "You are the Messiah, the Son of the living God."

Narrator: Jesus answered,

Jesus: "Good for you, Simon son of John! For this truth did not come to you from any human being, but it was given to you directly by my Father in heaven. And so I tell you, Peter: you are a rock, and on this rock foundation I will build my church."

Narrator: The gospel of the Lord.

All: Praise to you, Lord Jesus Christ.

Intercessions

Leader: We now offer our prayers and petitions to God. Our response is: Lord, hear our prayer.

Reader 1: May we be faithful followers of Jesus Christ all the days of our lives, we pray to the Lord.

All: Lord, hear our prayer.

Reader 2: May we always be true to the teachings of Jesus Christ, we pray to the Lord.

All: Lord, hear our prayer.

Reader 3: May we share the good news of Jesus Christ with others, we pray to the Lord.

All: Lord, hear our prayer.

Reader 4: May we reach out a helping hand to others in the name of Jesus Christ, we pray to the Lord.

All: Lord, hear our prayer.

Reader 5: May other people come to know Jesus Christ by the way we live our lives each day, we pray to the Lord.

All: Lord, hear our prayer.

Saint Peter

Saint Peter was the first apostle that Jesus called. He was a fisherman who left everything behind to follow Jesus.

Peter was a person of great faith and a leader in the early church. He told people the good news about Jesus Christ. We too are called to follow Jesus.

Duplicate the holy cards on colored card stock. Cut apart the cards and laminate them. Place in a basket.

Leader: All students are invited to come forward and take a St. Peter holy card from the basket as you leave. We are called to be people of faith as St. Peter was and to follow Jesus Christ in all things. (Allow students time to come forward and get a holy card.)

Closing Prayer

Leader: St. Peter knew in his heart that Jesus was our Savior and Redeemer. He preached the good news. We too are called to proclaim who Jesus Christ is to others. We are to live our lives as witnesses to all Jesus said and did.

All: Help us, Lord, to be people of faith like St. Peter. Amen.

Spring

The prayer services in this spring section will help the students journey through the Lent and Easter seasons together. These prayer services are for the months of March, April, and May. If the season of Lent comes early in a particular year, the Lenten prayer services in this section can be used earlier.

The season of Lent should be a time of prayer and a time of giving. It is a season of renewal and a time for growing in faith. We journey with Jesus to his life, death, and resurrection. Then we celebrate the glorious season of Easter as a time of hope and new life. God's promise to the people has been fulfilled in a way no one could have imagined. The church year helps us to celebrate all that God is and all that we are as God's people.

The prayer services at the beginning of this section will help students enter into the spirit of the Lenten season. Students are encouraged to lift up their hearts in prayer to our God and reach out to others. A reconciliation service is included to help the students celebrate this sacrament as a sign of God's forgiveness and mercy. The students will walk with Jesus Christ using the scriptural Stations of the Cross, which are based on the gospels. This is a meaningful experience for students, catechists, and parents. The students also learn about following Jesus Christ through prayer services honoring St. Katherine Drexel, St. Patrick, and Mary, the Mother of Jesus. With spring comes the beautiful Easter season which celebrates all that we believe. Prayer services are included to help the students give glory to God for the new life we have through Jesus Christ, our Lord and Savior.

Activities in each prayer service encourage the students to become involved. A Lenten giving tree is suggested as a way for students to reach out to people in need. A prayer cross helps students make Lent a time of prayer outside the classroom. Shamrock prayers invite the students to pray to God in their own words. Proclaiming the Annunciation in parts pulls the students into this gospel story and reminds them that we too are to say yes to God in our lives. The signs of new life for the Easter prayer table help the students give praise to God in this glorious season.

Renew Our hearts

Giving of Ourselves During Lent

Opening Prayer

· ·

Leader: During this holy season of Lent we are on a journey of faith to God the Father.

We are to live as Jesus Christ showed us with the help of the Holy Spirit. We must renew our hearts and turn toward God.

All: Lord, help us to do your will each day. Amen.

Litany

· ·

Leader: We reflect on the times when we have failed to love God and love others in our lives. Let us pray.

You call us to be people of prayer.

All: Lord, have mercy.

Leader: You call us to be people of peace.

All: Christ, have mercy.

Leader: You call us to be people of love.

All: Lord, have mercy.

First Reading

Reader.　　A reading from the book of Isaiah (58:6–8).

"The kind of fasting I want is this: Remove the chains of oppression and the yoke of injustice, and let the oppressed go free. Share your food with the hungry and open your homes to the homeless poor. Give clothes to those who have nothing to wear, and do not refuse to help your own relatives. Then my favor will shine on you like the morning sun."

The word of the Lord.

All:　　Thanks be to God.

Psalm Prayer (16:1–2, 11)

Leader:　　Let us pray together the words of our psalm.

All:　　Protect me, O God; I trust in you for safety.
I say to the Lord, "You are my Lord;
all the good things I have come from you."
You will show me the path that leads to life;
your presence fills me with joy
and brings me pleasure forever.

Gospel Reading

Gospel reader:

A reading from the holy gospel according to Mark (1:14–15).

Jesus went to Galilee and preached the Good News from God. "The right time has come," he said, "and the Kingdom of God is near! Turn away from your sins and believe the Good News!"

The gospel of the Lord.

All: Praise to you, Lord Jesus Christ.

Intercessions

Leader: During Lent we are to turn away from selfishness and toward God's love. Our response to each petition is: Lord, hear our prayer.

Reader 1:   For victims of war and violence, may they find peace and know that God is with them, we pray to the Lord.

All: Lord, hear our prayer.

Reader 2:   For people who have strayed from God, may they decide to come home to the Father, we pray to the Lord.

All: Lord, hear our prayer.

Reader 3:   For families facing a crisis, may they find strength in God and in one another, we pray to the Lord.

All: Lord, hear our prayer.

Reader 4:   For people in need of reconciliation, may they have the courage to ask forgiveness, we pray to the Lord.

All: Lord, hear our prayer.

Reader 5:   For all of us here today, during Lent may we renew our hearts and our lives, we pray to the Lord.

All: Lord, hear our prayer.

Leader: We ask you to hear these prayers and the prayers that we have left unspoken. Guide our hearts and our lives that we may be filled with your love.

All: Amen.

Lent Giving Tree

Encourage caring about others during Lent with a Lent giving tree. Prior to the prayer service, contact different organizations for what they need for the people they serve. Make paper crosses with each organization represented by a different color. For example, the items needed by a homeless shelter can be on green crosses, items needed by a children's program can be on blue crosses, and the items needed by a refugee organization can be on gold crosses. Use labels to put the specific items on the back. Punch holes on the top and hang the crosses on a potted tree branch using yarn.

Lenten Project

Leader: You are encouraged to come forward and take a cross from our Lent Giving Tree. On that cross is something needed by someone in our community. Each colored cross represents a different organization that helps people in need. We will be collecting items for the next two weeks. Please return the cross with your donation. We remember that Lent is a time of giving to others. (Students come forward to choose a cross and return to their places.)

Closing Prayer

Leader: God, Father and Creator,

help us to reach out to others

and to share your love with all people.

Renew our hearts and our lives that we may live as your people.

All: May we follow the example of your Son, Jesus Christ in serving others during Lent and always. Amen.

Take Up Your Cross

Living as Disciples During Lent

Opening Prayer

Leader: God, Father and Creator, during this holy season of Lent we gather together to remember all you have done for us. We thank you for your unending love for each of us. You sent your Son, Jesus Christ, to us as the Savior of the World. We give glory to your name through your Holy Spirit.

All: Amen.

First Reading

Reader: A reading from the book of Isaiah (42:1).

The Lord says, "Here is my servant, whom I strengthen— the one I have chosen with whom I am pleased. I have filled him with my Spirit, and he will bring justice to every nation."

The Word of the Lord.

All: Thanks be to God.

Psalm Prayer (138:1-5)

Leader: We now praise God with our psalm prayer.

Left: I thank you, Lord, with all my heart;
I sing praise to you before the gods,

Right: I face your holy Temple, bow down and praise your
name because of your constant love and faithfulness,

Left: Because you have shown that your name and your
commands are supreme.

Right: You answered me when I called to you; with your
strength you strengthened me.

Left: All the kings in the world will praise you, Lord, because
they have heard your promises.

Right: They will sing about what you have done and about your
great glory.

Gospel Reading

Gospel reader:

We listen to a reading from the holy gospel according to
Luke (9:23–25).

And Jesus said to them all, "If you want to come with
me, you must forget yourself, take up your cross every
day, and follow me. For if you want to save your own
life, you will lose it, but if you lose your life for my sake,
you will save it. Will you gain anything if you win the
whole world but are yourself lost?"

The gospel of the Lord.

All: Praise to you, Lord Jesus Christ.

Intercessions

Leader:	We remember today in our prayers those for whom life is difficult.
	Our response to each petition is: Lord, hear our prayer.
Reader 1:	For those who carry the cross of poverty, may they find a helping hand, we pray to the Lord.
All:	Lord, hear our prayer.
Reader 2:	For those who carry the cross of injustice, may they be treated fairly, we pray to the Lord.
All:	Lord, hear our prayer.
Reader 3:	For those who carry the cross of sickness, may they be comforted, we pray to the Lord.
All:	Lord, hear our prayer.
Reader 4:	For those who carry the cross of war, may they find peace, we pray to the Lord.
All:	Lord, hear our prayer.
Reader 5:	For those who carry the cross of mental illness, may they be healed, we pray to the Lord.
All:	Lord, hear our prayer.
Leader:	We ask you, Lord, to hear our prayers and our petitions. We pray for all those in need around the world. Be with them and guide them as they struggle to carry their crosses each day. Amen.

Lent Prayer Cross

Lent Prayer

Jesus, during this holy season of Lent, we ask you to be with us.

Help us to follow you always.

May we live in justice and walk in peace.

Amen

Duplicate on purple copy paper and laminate. Cut out the crosses and place them in a basket.

Leader: Come forward at this time to get a Lent prayer cross. We will pray this prayer now and you can pray it at home with your family during this season of Lent. (Each student takes a prayer cross from the basket.)

Closing Prayer

All: Jesus, during this holy season of Lent,
we ask you to be with us.
Help us to follow you always.
May we live in justice
and walk in peace. Amen.

Life of Love

Remembering St. Katherine Drexel

Opening Prayer

· ·

Leader: We remember today the example of St. Katherine Drexel. She was concerned for the poor and oppressed people living in the United States. She saw the face of Jesus in each person she met. Her life reminds us to treat all persons with dignity and respect.

All: Lord God, open our minds and hearts to your will in our lives.

Help us to live in peace and work for justice. Amen.

First Reading

· ·

Reader: A reading from the book of Ezekiel (36:26–28).

I will give you a new heart and a new mind. I will take away your stubborn heart of stone and give you an obedient heart. I will put my spirit in you and will see to it that you follow my laws and keep all the commands I have given you. Then you will live in the land I gave your ancestors. You will be my people, and I will be your God.

The word of the Lord.

All: Thanks be to God.

Psalm Prayer (70:4)

Leader: We pray the words of our psalm prayer together.

All: May all who come to you be glad and joyful. May all who are thankful for your salvation always say, "How great is God!"

Gospel Reading

Gospel reader:

A reading from the holy gospel according to Luke (6:37).

Jesus said, "Do not judge others, and God will not judge you; do not condemn others and God will not condemn you; forgive others, and God will forgive you. Give to others and God will give to you."

The gospel of the Lord.

All: Praise to you, Lord Jesus Christ

Reflection

St. Katherine Drexel devoted her life to serving God and others. She founded many schools and missions in the United States. She reached out to children, orphans, and the sick. She helped wherever there was a need. St. Katherine worked against racism and for justice for all people. She had a great devotion to Jesus Christ in the eucharist. She knew that receiving the eucharist was a promise to treat all people as our brothers and sisters. We should follow her example.

After School Snacks for the Family Shelter

Collect after school snacks for the local family or women's shelter. Explain to the children that families staying at a shelter do not have the means to provide snacks for hungry children in the afternoon. Send home a letter to the families asking for their cooperation and support.

Ask for snacks that are single servings and prepackaged. Students can bring their contribution to the prayer service and place the snacks in a marked box.

Leader: Thank you for bringing after school snacks for the children at the family shelter. We are called to reach out to other people in the name of our Lord Jesus Christ. Please bring your donations forward at this time. (Allow students to come forward with their items for the collection box.)

Intercessions

Leader:	Together we offer our prayers to the Lord. Our response is: Lord, hear our prayer.
Reader 1:	May we always remember that all people are created in God's image, we pray to the Lord.
All:	Lord, hear our prayer.
Reader 2:	May we have the courage to live in peace in our communities, our nations, and our world, we pray to the Lord.
All:	Lord, hear our prayer.
Reader 3:	May there be an end to discrimination and racism, we pray to the Lord.
All:	Lord, hear our prayer.
Reader 4:	May victims of war and violence find peace in their lives, we pray to the Lord.
All:	Lord, hear our prayer.
Reader 5:	May world leaders put aside differences and work together for the good of all people, we pray to the Lord.
All:	Lord, hear our prayer.
Reader 6:	May we become bread for others and give them what they need, we pray to the Lord.

All: Lord, hear our prayer.

Leader: We ask you, Lord, to help us live as you showed us.
Guide our hearts and our lives.

All: Amen.

Closing Prayer

Leader: Father of us all,
you give us the gift of your Son, Jesus Christ,
in the eucharist out of love.
Help us to know that sharing in the eucharist
means being united not only with Jesus Christ,
but with one another.
Help us to care about others and reach out
in your name to people in need.

All: Amen.

Patron of Ireland

Celebrating St. Patrick

Opening Prayer

Leader: Lord Jesus Christ, we gather together to hear your Word in scripture. Help us to live what we hear proclaimed. As we celebrate the example of St. Patrick, may we remember that we also are called to follow you.

All: Jesus Christ, you are Lord for ever and ever. Amen.

First Reading

Reader: A reading from the letter of Paul to the Philippians (1:3–6).

I thank my God for you every time I think of you; and every time I pray for you all, I pray with joy because of the way in which you have helped me in the work of the gospel from the very first day until now. And so I am sure that God, who began this good work in you, will carry it on until it is finished on the Day of Christ Jesus.

The word of the Lord.

All: Thanks be to God.

Psalm Prayer (117)

Leader: Let us praise God with our psalm.

All: Praise the Lord, all nations! Praise him, all peoples!

His love for us is strong, and his faithfulness is eternal.

Praise the Lord!

Gospel Reading

Gospel reader:

A reading from the holy gospel according to Matthew (28:18–20).

Jesus drew near and said to them, "I have been given all authority in heaven and on earth. Go, then, to all peoples everywhere and make them my disciples: baptize them in the name of the Father, the Son, and the Holy Spirit, and teach them to obey everything I have commanded you. And I will be with you always, to the end of the age."

The gospel of the Lord.

All: Praise to you, Lord Jesus Christ.

Reflection

St. Patrick went to Ireland to teach the people the good news about Jesus Christ. He explained the Trinity using a shamrock which grows wild in that country. He said that just as the one shamrock has three leaves so one God is three persons. Father, Son, and Holy Spirit. He went all over Ireland preaching, baptizing people, and building churches. We too are called to share the good news of God's love with others.

Shamrock Prayers

To prepare for the prayer service copy four shamrocks to a page of green paper. Cut apart in squares. In class explain how St. Patrick used the shamrock to explain the Trinity. Talk about praying for our needs, for family and friends, and for others we don't know. Give each student a shamrock on which to write a short prayer to God of what is in their hearts. The students bring their shamrock prayers to the prayer service.

Leader: You are now invited to come forward with your shamrock prayers and place them in the basket on our prayer table. The shamrock reminds us of our God who hears all our prayers. (Students come forward with their shamrock prayers.)

Shamrock Prayer

Litany Prayer

Leader: We now ask St. Patrick to pray for us to the Lord our God.

Our response is: "pray for us."

Litany reader:

St. Patrick, missionary to the people . . . pray for us.

Litany reader:

St. Patrick, patron saint of Ireland . . . pray for us.

Litany reader:

St. Patrick, person of courage . . . pray for us.

Litany reader:

St. Patrick, builder of churches . . . pray for us.

Litany reader:

St. Patrick, witness to the gospel . . . pray for us.

Leader: Jesus Christ, hear the prayers of your servant, St. Patrick, and the prayers that we offer to you each day. Amen.

Closing Blessing

Leader: We go now to live as God's followers each day as did St. Patrick. We ask God's blessing on us and on all that we do in the name of the Father, and of the Son, and of the Holy Spirit.

All: Amen.

Annunciation of the Lord

Honoring the Blessed Mother

Display a statue of Mary on a small table in the area where the prayer service will be held. Underneath the statue place a blue cloth. Place a vase of flowers in front of the statue.

Opening Prayer

Leader: Today we celebrate the feast of the Annunciation of the Lord. We honor Mary who followed the will of God all her life. She said yes to what God asked of her. Mary is a model of faith for all of us.

All: We honor you, Mary, as the Mother of God and our mother too. Amen.

First Reading

Reader: A reading from the Revelation to John (12:1, 5).

Then a great and mysterious sight appeared in the sky. There was a woman, whose dress was the sun and who had the moon under her feet and a crown of twelve stars on her head . . . She gave birth to a son, who will rule over all nations with an iron rod. But the child was snatched away and taken to God and his throne.

The word of the Lord.

All: Thanks be to God.

Psalm Prayer (8:1)

Leader: Let us pray words of praise to our God.

All: O Lord, our Lord,
            your greatness is seen in all the world!
            Your praise reaches up to the heavens.

Gospel Reading

(Before the prayer service, ask for volunteers to read the parts of the narrator, the angel, and Mary. This dramatic reading brings the gospel alive for students.)

Narrator: A reading from the holy gospel according to Luke (1:26–38).

            In the sixth month of Elizabeth's pregnancy God sent the angel Gabriel to a town in Galilee named Nazareth. He had a message for a young woman promised in marriage to a man named Joseph, who was a descendant of King David. Her name was Mary. The angel came to her and said,

Angel: Peace be with you! The Lord is with you and has greatly blessed you!

Narrator: Mary was deeply troubled by the angel's message, and she wondered what his words meant. The angel said to her,

Angel: Don't be afraid, Mary; God has been gracious to you. You will become pregnant and give birth to a son, and you will name him Jesus. He will be great and will be called the Son of the Most High God. The Lord God will make him a king, as his ancestor David was, and he will be the king of the descendants of Jacob forever; his kingdom will never end!

Narrator: Mary said to the angel,

Mary: I am a virgin. How, then, can this be?

Narrator: The angel answered,

Angel: The Holy Spirit will come on you, and God's power will rest on you. For this reason the holy child will be called the Son of God. Remember your relative Elizabeth. It is said that she cannot have children, but she herself is now six months pregnant, even though she is very old. For there is nothing God cannot do.

Narrator: Mary said,

Mary: I am the Lord's servant, may it happen to me as you have said.

Narrator: The gospel of the Lord.

All: Praise to you, Lord Jesus Christ.

Intercessions

Leader: We ask Mary for her prayers that she may intercede with God for us.

Our response is:

Mary, Mother of God, pray for us.

Reader 1:   Mary was the Mother of Jesus. May we also bring Jesus into the world for others.

All: Mary, Mother of God, pray for us.

Reader 2:   Mary lived a life pleasing to God. May we do God's will in all things.

All: Mary, Mother of God, pray for us.

Reader 3:   Mary gave glory to God through her life. May we give praise to God in all we do.

All: Mary, Mother of God, pray for us.

Reader 4:   Mary was a holy person. May we strive to live as God created us.

All: Mary, Mother of God, pray for us.

Reader 5:   Mary was a person of courage. May we do what we know is right.

All: Mary, Mother of God, pray for us.

Hail Mary

Leader: Let us pray together the Hail Mary.

All: Hail Mary, full of grace the Lord is with you.
Blessed are you among women
and blessed is the fruit of your womb, Jesus.
Holy Mary, Mother of God, pray for us sinners
now and at the hour of our death. Amen

Closing Prayer

Leader: Mary was always faithful to God's will. She was faithful at the stable in Bethlehem, she was faithful on the flight to Egypt, and she was faithful at the foot of the cross. We should follow her example and be faithful to God's will in our lives.

All: Father, help us to do your will even when it is difficult. We ask this through our Lord Jesus Christ and your Holy Spirit. Amen.

God of Mercy

Celebrating a Reconciliation Service

Sacrament of Reconciliation

This service includes the opportunity for individual reception of the sacrament of reconciliation from a priest. Set up stations around the church with two chairs and a table at each one. Avoid long lines during the service by asking the students to wait in their pews until there is a priest available.

Introductory Rites

Greeting

Presider: We come together as the people of God. We celebrate our God who is a God of mercy and a God of forgiveness. God's love for us is without boundaries and without end. We ask God to have mercy on us.

All: Father of us all, we give you glory for ever and ever.

Presider: God has given us the gift of the sacrament of reconciliation. Through this sacrament we are called to be reconciled with God and with one another. Our God is a loving Father who always welcomes us back.

All: Father of all, help us to live as your people.

Opening Prayer

Presider: Lord God, hear our prayer. We come before you and ask for your forgiveness. Sometimes we do not live the greatest commandment as Jesus taught us. We do not live in love of God and love of others. We ask you to grant us your forgiveness and help us to find our way back to you.

All: Father, help us to turn away from sin and toward the light of your love. Amen.

Celebration of the Word of God

Gospel

(For proclaiming this gospel in parts the Presider is the narrator. Students read the parts of the younger son, the older son, and the father.)

Presider: A reading from the holy gospel according to Luke (15:11–14, 17–24, 28–29, 31–32).

Jesus went on to say,

"There was once a man who had two sons. The younger one said to him,

Younger son:

'Father, give me my share of the property now.'

Presider: So the man divided his property between his two sons. After a few days the younger son sold his part of the property and left home with the money. He went to a country far away, where he wasted his money in reckless living. He spent everything he had. . . . At last he came to his senses and said,

Younger son:

> 'All my father's hired workers have more than they can eat, and here I am about to starve! I will get up and go to my father and say, "Father, I have sinned against God and against you. I am no longer fit to be called your son; treat me as one of your hired workers."'

Presider: So he got up and started back to his father. He was still a long way from home when his father saw him; his heart was filled with pity, and he ran, threw his arms around his son, and kissed him. The son said,

Younger son:

> 'Father, I have sinned against God and against you. I am no longer fit to be called your son.'

Presider: But the father called to his servants,

Father: 'Hurry! Bring the best robe and put it on him. Put a ring on his finger and shoes on his feet. Then go and get the prize calf and kill it, and let us celebrate with a feast! For this son of mine was dead, but now he is alive; he was lost, but now he has been found.'

Presider: The older brother was so angry that he would not go into the house; so his father came out and begged him to come in. But he spoke back to his father,

Older brother:

> 'Look, all these years I have worked for you like a slave, and I have never disobeyed your orders. What have you given me?'

Presider: The Father answered,

Father: 'My son, you are always here with me, and everything I have is yours. But we had to celebrate and be happy, because your brother was dead, but now he is alive; he was lost, but now he has been found.'"

Presider: The gospel of the Lord.

All: Praise to you, Lord Jesus Christ.

Homily

· ·

The presider talks briefly to the students about the gospel reading and our need to give and ask forgiveness.

Examination of Conscience

· ·

Presider: There are times when we have chosen the wrong path. Let us now think about our actions that have separated us from God and from one another. Our response is: Forgive us, Lord.

Reader: For the times when we were selfish and did not think of others,

All: Forgive us, Lord.

Reader: For the times when we did not pray,

All: Forgive us, Lord.

Reader: For the times when we treated other people unfairly,

All: Forgive us, Lord.

Reader: For the times when we took something that was not ours to keep,

All: Forgive us, Lord.

Reader: For the times when we did not ask forgiveness of other people,

All: Forgive us, Lord.

Reader: For the times when we failed to use our gifts and talents for the good of others,

All: Forgive us, Lord.

Reader: For the times when we did not trust in your mercy,

All: Forgive us, Lord.

Presider: God, we ask forgiveness for all our sins. May we be truly sorry for the things we have done wrong and the good things we did not do. Help us to live as your people each day. May we be people of forgiveness.

All: Amen.

Rite of Reconciliation

Presider: Let us now pray together the prayer that Jesus taught us.

All: Our Father . . .

Individual Confession and Absolution

Presider: The priests will now move to their stations. You may go to the priest of your choice for the sacrament of reconciliation when you are ready. Please stay in your pew until a priest is available rather than forming lines.

Concluding Prayer of Thanksgiving

Presider: We are called to change our lives and live as Jesus Christ taught us. We are to live in the Father's forgiveness and love. We ask the Holy Spirit to guide our lives and our hearts.

All: Be with us in all things. Amen.

Concluding Rite

Presider: May almighty God bless you, in the name of the Father, and the Son, and the Holy Spirit.

All: Amen.

Dismissal

Presider: Our God is forgiving and merciful. We are to share God's forgiveness and peace with others. Go now to live in peace in your family, your community, and your world.

All: Thanks be to God.

Walking With Jesus

Praying the Scriptural Stations of the Cross

Ask for fifteen students to volunteer to each read the scripture at one of the stations. Print out the response for the rest of the students on quarter sheets of paper. The leader can gesture with one hand to indicate when it is time to pray the response at each station. Everyone may sit during the scripture readings and stand for dialogue between the leader and all.

Opening

· ·

Leader: Tonight we will walk the way of the cross remembering how Jesus made the final journey to his death and resurrection. We remember all that Jesus Christ has done for us. The response at each station is:

Jesus, may we walk in faith, hope, and love each day.

Turn our hearts and lives toward your kingdom.

Leader: The First Station, Jesus Prays in the Garden of Olives

Reader: Then Jesus went with his disciples to a place called Gethsemane, and he said to them, "Sit here while I go over there and pray." He took with him Peter and the two sons of Zebedee. Grief and anguish came over him, and he said to them, "The sorrow in my heart is so great that it almost crushes me. Stay here and keep watch with me." He went a little farther on, threw himself face downward on the ground, and prayed, "My Father, if it is possible, take this cup of suffering from me! Yet not what

I want, but what you want." Then he returned to the three disciples and found them asleep; and he said to Peter, "How is it that you three were not able to keep watch with me for even one hour?" (Matthew 26:36–40)

Leader: Jesus prayed because he knew what was ahead for him. But he accepted the Father's will. We too are to be people of prayer and pray for our needs and the needs of others.

All: Jesus, may we walk in faith, hope, and love each day. Turn our hearts and our lives toward your kingdom.

Leader: The Second Station, Jesus Is Betrayed by Judas

Reader: Jesus was still speaking when Judas, one of the twelve disciples, arrived. With him was a crowd armed with swords and clubs and sent by the chief priests, the teachers of the Law, and the elders. The traitor had given the crowd a signal: "The man I kiss is the one you want. Arrest him and take him away under guard." As soon as Judas arrived, he went up to Jesus and said, "Teacher!" and kissed him. So they arrested Jesus and held him tight. (Mark 14:43–46)

Leader: Jesus must have been deeply hurt by the betrayal of Judas. We must be careful of how we treat other people in our lives. We must ask forgiveness of those we have hurt by our actions or our words.

All: Jesus, may we walk in faith, hope, and love each day. Turn our hearts and lives toward your kingdom.

Leader: The Third Station, Jesus Is Condemned by the Sanhedrin

Reader: When the day came… Jesus was brought before the Council. "Tell us," they said, "are you the Messiah?" He answered, "If I tell you, you will not believe me; and if I ask you a question, you will not answer. But from now on the Son of Man will be seated at the right side of Almighty God. " They all said, "Are you, then, the Son of God?" He answered them, "You say that I am." And they said, "We don't need any witnesses! We ourselves have heard what he said!" (Luke 22:66–71)

Leader: We know in our hearts that Jesus is the Messiah and the Son of God. We must publicly proclaim our faith in God and stand up for what we believe. We must have the courage to do what is right.

All: Jesus, may we walk in faith, hope, and love each day. Turn our hearts and lives toward your kingdom.

Leader: The Fourth Station, Jesus Is Denied By Peter

Reader: Peter was sitting outside in the courtyard when one of the High Priest's servant women came to him and said, "You, too, were with Jesus of Galilee." But he denied it in front of them all. "I don't know what you are talking about," he answered. (Matthew 26:69–70)

Leader: Peter denied that he knew Jesus three times, but Jesus forgave him. Peter became a person of great faith and the leader of the church. We must remember that Jesus will always forgive us.

All: Jesus, may we walk in faith, hope, and love each day. Turn our hearts and lives toward your kingdom.

Leader: The Fifth Station, Jesus Is Judged by Pilate

Reader: Pilate spoke again to the crowd, "What, then, do you want me to do with the one you call the king of the Jews?" They shouted back, "Crucify him!" "But what crime has he committed?" Pilate asked. They shouted all the louder, "Crucify him!" Pilate wanted to please the crowd, so he set Barabbas free for them. Then he had Jesus whipped. (Mark 15:12–15)

Leader: We must stand up for what is right even when it is not easy. We should ask God's help to make good decisions in our lives. God is with us in all that we do.

All: Jesus, may we walk in faith, hope, and love each day. Turn our hearts and lives toward your kingdom.

Leader: The Sixth Station, Jesus Is Crowned With Thorns

Reader: The soldiers made a crown of thorny branches and put it on his head; then they put a purple robe on him and came to him and said, "Long live the King of the Jews!" And they went up and slapped him. (John 19:2–3)

Leader: Jesus was forced to wear a crown of thorns and suffered terribly. We should remember all that Jesus did out of love for us. All around our world people are treated unjustly. We must work for justice and peace.

All: Jesus, may we walk in faith, hope, and love each day. Turn our hearts and lives toward your kingdom.

Leader: The Seventh Station, Jesus Carries the Cross

Reader: Then Pilate handed Jesus over to them to be crucified. So they took charge of Jesus. He went out, carrying his cross, and came to "The Place of the Skull," as it is called. (John 19:16–17)

Leader: Jesus was unjustly treated as a criminal. But he did what he had to do. He picked up his cross and walked toward his death. We must walk in love all our lives as Jesus taught us by his word and his example.

All: Jesus, may we walk in faith, hope, and love each day. Turn our hearts and lives toward your kingdom.

Leader: The Eighth Station, Jesus Is Helped By Simon of Cyrene

Reader: As they were going out, they met a man from Cyrene named Simon, and the soldiers forced him to carry Jesus' cross. (Matthew 27:32)

Leader: Simon was made to help Jesus carry his cross. We too must step forward from the crowd to help people in need. All around our world people carry the cross of hatred and discrimination. We should work for the good of all people.

All: Jesus, may we walk in faith, hope, and love each day. Turn our hearts and lives toward your kingdom.

Leader: The Ninth Station, Jesus Meets the Women of Jerusalem

Reader: A large crowd of people followed Jesus; among them were some women who were weeping and wailing for him. Jesus turned to them and said, "Women of Jerusalem! Don't cry for me, but for yourselves and your children." (Luke 23:27–28)

Leader: In spite of his suffering, Jesus stops to talk to the women. Jesus told the women not to weep for him. We should treat others with kindness in the name of Jesus. We are called to walk in love all our lives as Jesus taught us.

All: Jesus, may we walk in faith, hope, and love each day. Turn our hearts and lives toward your kingdom.

Leader: The Tenth Station, Jesus Is Crucified

Reader: They took Jesus to a place called Golgotha. . . Then they crucified him and divided his clothes among themselves, throwing dice to see who would get which piece of clothing. It was nine o'clock in the morning when they crucified him. The notice of the accusation against him said, "The King of the Jews." (Mark 15:22, 24–26)

Leader: On Good Friday Jesus was crucified for our sins. He had done nothing wrong. We remember all that Jesus did for love of us.

All: Jesus, may we walk in faith, hope, and love each day. Turn our hearts and lives toward your kingdom.

Leader: The Eleventh Station, Jesus Speaks to the Thief

Reader: One of the criminals hanging there hurled insults at Jesus: "Aren't you the Messiah? Save yourself and us!" The other one, however, rebuked him, saying, "Don't you fear God? You received that same sentence he did. Ours, however, is only right, because we are getting what we deserve for what we did; but he has done no wrong."

And he said to Jesus, "Remember me, Jesus, when you come as King!" Jesus said to him, "I promise you that today you will be in Paradise with me." (Luke 23:39–43)

Leader: We must believe in Jesus as the did the thief on the cross. We should accept the gift of Jesus' forgiveness which is offered to all of us. And we must grant forgiveness to the people who have hurt us.

All: Jesus, may we walk in faith, hope, and love each day. Turn our hearts and lives toward your kingdom.

Leader: The Twelfth Station, Jesus Speaks to His Mother

Reader: Standing close to Jesus' cross were his mother, his mother's sister, Mary the wife of Clopas, and Mary Magdalene. Jesus saw his mother and the disciple he loved standing there; so he said to his mother, " He is your son." Then he said to the disciple, "She is your mother." (John 19:25–27)

Leader: Mary saw her son crucified as a criminal. How that must have hurt her. And yet she was faithful to God all her life. We too must be faithful followers of Jesus even when the going gets tough.

All: Jesus, may we walk in faith, hope, and love each day. Turn our hearts and lives toward your kingdom.

Leader: The Thirteenth Station, Jesus Dies on the Cross

Reader: It was about twelve o'clock when the sun stopped shining and darkness covered the whole country until three o'clock; and the curtain hanging in the Temple was torn in two. Jesus cried out in a loud voice, "Father! In your hands I place my spirit!" He said this and died. (Luke: 23:44–46)

Leader: Jesus died a terrible death for all of us. Such is the depth of God's unending love. We must open our hearts and our lives to all God has done for us.

All: Jesus, may we walk in faith, hope, and love each day. Turn our hearts and lives toward your kingdom.

Leader: The Fourteenth Station, Jesus Is Placed in the Tomb

Reader: It was toward evening when Joseph of Arimathea. . . went boldly into the presence of Pilate and asked him for the body of Jesus. Pilate was surprised to hear that Jesus was already dead. . . Pilate told Joseph he could have the body. Joseph brought a linen sheet, took the body down, wrapped it in the sheet, and placed it in a tomb which had been dug out of solid rock. Then he rolled a large stone across the entrance to the tomb. (Mark 15:42–46)

Leader: Jesus died that he might be raised to new life. We are to keep the hope of the resurrection alive in our hearts. We must tell the good news of God's love to others.

All: Jesus, may we walk in faith, hope, and love each day. Turn our hearts and lives toward your kingdom.

Leader: The Fifteenth Station, Jesus Is Raised From the Dead

Reader: Very early on Sunday morning the women went to the tomb, carrying the spices they had prepared. They found the stone rolled away from the entrance to the tomb, so they went in; but they did not find the body of the Lord Jesus. They stood there puzzled about this, when suddenly two men in bright shining clothes stood by them. Full of fear, the women bowed down to the ground, as the men said to them "Why are you looking among the dead for one who is alive? He is not here; he has been raised. (Luke 24:1–6)

Leader: We die and rise with Christ. Jesus brings new life to all of us through his life, death, and resurrection. The story is not over, it is just beginning. We are an Easter people; a people of hope.

All: Jesus, may we walk in faith, hope, and love each day. Turn our hearts and lives toward your kingdom.

Closing

Leader: Jesus Christ, you are our Lord and Savior. You showed us the depth of your love by walking the way of the cross to your death and resurrection. Help us to follow you each day. May all that we say and all that we do give glory to your name.

All: Amen.

Signs of Easter

Rejoicing in the New Life of Easter

Opening Prayer

Leader: God, you are Father, Son, and Holy Spirit. We come before you in this glorious Easter season to celebrate all that you have done out of love for us. We praise you for the life, death, and resurrection of Jesus Christ, our Lord and Redeemer.

All: Jesus has brought us new life. Amen. Alleluia.

Easter Symbols

Before the prayer service ask five volunteers to carry symbols of hope. Give the first student a white cloth, the second student a gold cross, the third student a blooming marigold in a pot, the fourth student a budding branch taken from a tree, and the fifth student a colorful paper butterfly.

Leader: We celebrate Easter in the springtime when life is renewed. We now bring forward symbols of the new life that Jesus Christ brings us and place them on our prayer table.

             We place a white cloth on our prayer table as a sign of a world made new in Christ.

             (Student lays the cloth across the table.)

We place a gold cross on our prayer table because it is through the life, death, and resurrection of Jesus Christ that we are redeemed.

(Student places the cross in the center of the table.)

We place a blooming plant on our prayer table as a sign that Jesus Christ has risen and Easter has come.

(Student puts the marigold on the right side prayer table.)

We place a budding branch on the table because in the spring we praise God for new life.

(Student puts the branch on the left side of the table.)

We place a butterfly on the table to remind us that each of us shares in the resurrection of Jesus Christ.

(Student puts the butterfly in front of the cross on the table.)

Leader: Let us pray together.

All: Thank you, God, for sending Jesus Christ to us and for the new life he brings to our world. Help us to remember all that you have done out of love for us. Alleluia.

First Reading

Reader: A reading from the letter of Paul to the Ephesians (1:18–20).

I ask that your minds may be opened to see his light, so that you will know what is the hope to which he has called you, how rich are the wonderful blessings he promises his people, and how very great is his power at work in us who believe. This power working in us is the same as the mighty strength which he used when he raised Christ from death and seated him as his right side in the heavenly world.

The word of the Lord.

All: Thanks be to God.

Psalm Prayer (86:9–12)

Leader: We offer our psalm of praise to our God.

Left: All the nations that you have created
            will come and bow down to you;
            they will praise your greatness.

Right: You are mighty and do wonderful things;
            you alone are God.

Left: Teach me, Lord, what you want me to do,
            and I will obey you faithfully;
            teach me to serve you with complete devotion.

Right: I will praise you with all my heart, O Lord my God;
            I will proclaim your greatness forever.

Gospel Reading

Gospel reader:

            A reading from the holy gospel according to Matthew
            (28:1–2, 5–6).

            After the Sabbath, as Sunday morning was dawning,
            Mary Magdalene and the other Mary went to look at the
            tomb. Suddenly there was a violent earthquake; an angel
            of the Lord came down from heaven, rolled the stone
            away, and sat on it. . . . The angel spoke to the women.
            "You must not be afraid," he said. "I know you are
            looking for Jesus, who was crucified. He is not here; he
            has been raised, just as he said."

            The gospel of the Lord.

All: Praise to you, Lord Jesus Christ.

Easter Litany

Leader: We offer our prayers and petitions. Our response is: Risen Savior, hear our prayer.

Reader 1: For missionaries in other lands, may they carry the good news to those who have not yet heard of Jesus Christ.

All: Risen Savior, hear our prayer.

Reader 2: For leaders of all nations, may they learn to live in peace with one another.

All: Risen Savior, hear our prayer.

Reader 3: For all those who live in poverty, may people share with them so they will have what they need.

All: Risen Savior, hear our prayer.

Reader 4: For those who are sick or in the hospital, may they find comfort in the healing presence of God.

All: Risen Savior, hear our prayer.

Reader 5: For our church, may we reach out to welcome all people in the name of our Savior.

All: Risen Savior, hear our prayer.

Leader: Lord, hear our prayers this day that we may be strengthened to live as you have shown us. We ask this through your Holy Spirit of love. Amen.

Closing Prayer

Left: Father, you are the source of all wisdom and love.

Right: We thank you for sending your Son, Jesus Christ, to us as teacher and savior.

Left: Through his life, death, and resurrection we are redeemed.

Right: May we live in faith, hope, and love as Easter people.

Left: Fill our hearts and our lives with the joy of this holy Easter season.

Right: We ask the Holy Spirit to guide our lives that we may walk with the risen Christ.

All: Amen.

Road to Emmaus

Celebrating the Easter Season

Opening Prayer

· ·

Leader: In this holy Easter season we gather together in the presence of God and one another. We remember all that God has done for us. We thank God for our many blessings.

All: Alleluia!

Leader: All of us have new life with Jesus Christ through his death and resurrection. He came to redeem us and show us how to live. We pray that we will be faithful followers of Jesus Christ in all that we do.

All: Alleluia!

Leader: God sent the Holy Spirit to us so that we may live in Christ. In the waters of baptism we are reborn as children of God. We pray that we will live always as people of hope.

All: Alleluia!

First Reading

· ·

Reader: A reading from the letter of Paul to the Ephesians (1:3–4).

Let us give thanks to the God and Father of our Lord Jesus Christ! For in our union with Christ he has blessed us by giving us every spiritual blessing in the heavenly world. Even before the world was made, God had already chosen us to be his through our union with Christ, so that we would be holy and without fault before him.

The word of the Lord.

All: Thanks be to God.

Psalm Prayer (118:28-29)

· ·

Leader: We now give praise to the Lord together with our psalm prayer.

All: You are my God, and I give you thanks;
        I will proclaim your greatness.

        Give thanks to the Lord, because he is good,
        and his love is eternal.

Gospel Reading

· ·

(Before the prayer service, ask for volunteers to read the parts of the narrator, Cleopas, and the follower. This dramatic reading brings the gospel alive for students.)

Narrator: This is a reading from the holy gospel according to Luke 24:13–35.

        On that same day two of Jesus' followers were going to a village named Emmaus, about seven miles from Jerusalem, and they were talking to each other about all the things that had happened. As they talked and discussed, Jesus himself drew near and walked along with them; they saw him, but somehow did not recognize him. Jesus said to them,

Jesus: "What are you talking about to each other, as you walk along?"

Narrator:	They stood still, with sad faces. One of them, named Cleopas, asked him,
Cleopas:	"Are you the only visitor in Jerusalem who doesn't not know the things that have been happening there these last few days?"
Jesus:	"What things?"
Cleopas:	"The things that happened to Jesus of Nazareth. This man was a prophet and was considered by God and by all the people to be powerful in everything he said and did. Our chief priests and rulers handed him over to be sentenced to death, and he was crucified. And we had hoped that he would be the one who was going to set Israel free!"
Follower:	"Besides all that, this is now the third day since it happened. Some of the women of our group surprised us; they went at dawn to the tomb, but could not find his body. They came back saying they had seen a vision of angels who told them that he is alive. Some of our group went to the tomb and found it exactly as the women had said, but they did not see him."
Narrator:	Then Jesus said to them,
Jesus:	"How foolish you are, how slow you are to believe everything the prophets said! Was it not necessary for the Messiah to suffer these things and then to enter his glory?"
Narrator:	And Jesus explained to them what was said about himself in all the Scriptures, beginning with the book of Moses and the writings of all the prophets. As they came near the village to which they were going, Jesus acted as if he were going farther; but they held him back, saying,
Cleopas:	"Stay with us; the day is almost over and it is getting dark."
Narrator:	So he went in to stay with them. He sat down to eat with them, took the bread and said the blessing; then he broke the bread and gave it to them. Then their eyes were

opened and they recognized him, but he disappeared from their sight. They said to each other,

Cleopas: "Wasn't it like a fire burning in us when he talked to us on the road and explained the Scriptures to us?"

Narrator: They got up at once and went back to Jerusalem, where they found the eleven disciples gathered together with the others and saying, "The Lord is risen indeed! He has appeared to Simon!" The two then explained to them what had happened on the road, and how they had recognized the Lord when he broke the bread.

The gospel of the Lord.

All: Praise to you, Lord, Jesus Christ.

Intercessions

Leader: We offer our prayers to the Lord who walks with us on our journey each day.

Our response is:

Lord, hear our prayer.

Reader 1: May we be like Mary Magdalene who recognized the presence of the risen Christ in her life.

All: Lord, hear our prayer.

Reader 2: May we be like the apostles who proclaimed, "We have seen the Lord."

All: Lord, hear our prayer.

Reader 3: May we be like Thomas who declared that Jesus Christ is our Lord and our God.

All: Lord, hear our prayer.

Reader 4: May we be like Peter who was confirmed in faith and shared the good news with others.

All: Lord, hear our prayer.

Reader 5:   May we be like the two on the road to Emmaus who knew Jesus in the word and in the eucharist,

All: Lord, hear our prayer.

Leader: Lord, hear our prayers that we may live as Easter people in all things.

All: Amen.

Closing Prayer

Leader: God of all, help us live always in the hope of the Easter season. May we share the good news of the Father's love with others and carry on the mission of Jesus Christ to the world. May we live each day with an Easter faith and rejoice in the new life of Jesus Christ, who is our Lord and Savior. We ask this through your Holy Spirit of love.

All: Amen. Alleluia.

Summer

The prayer services in the summer section will help the students celebrate the presence of God in their lives, Father, Son, and Holy Spirit. These prayer services reflect what is going on in the year during June, July, and August and speak to the experiences of students. During summer it is important not to take a vacation from prayer. The prayer services in this section can be used in the increasingly popular summer programs. If the students do not meet during this time, the prayer services can be used at various times during the rest of the year.

The feast of Pentecost is the birthday of the church. The Spirit comes to each of us to guide our hearts and our church. After Pentecost we return to Ordinary Time. We remember that we are called to follow Jesus Christ in all that we do. We hear gospel stories that proclaim how we are to live as Christians.

A prayer service to the Holy Spirit begins this section to help the students celebrate Pentecost and the Holy Spirit at work in our lives. Another prayer service calls us to live the greatest commandment, to love God and others in our lives. This is what it means to be a disciples of Jesus Christ. A prayer service honoring St. Thomas helps students to proclaim their own faith in God. The final prayer service explores the idea that we are called to walk in justice and reach out to others in the name of Jesus Christ.

Activities in each prayer service involve the students in exploring what it means to be a disciple of Jesus Christ. Holy Spirit prayer cards remind them to live in the Spirit. Presenting bibles to the students helps them learn to live the gospels in their lives. A collection for refugee families encourages students and families to reach out to others. A "Hearts for Jesus" activity encourages the students to live in love each day. All the students work together on a prayer chain that includes prayers for others. We are to be people of prayer in all things.

Living in the Spirit

Celebrating Pentecost

Opening Prayer

Leader: We celebrate the feast of Pentecost as the birthday of our church. The same Holy Spirit who came to the apostles lives in our church today. We are to be people of the Holy Spirit in all that we do.

All: Come, Holy Spirit, into our hearts and our lives. Amen.

First Reading

Reader: The story of Pentecost from the Acts of the Apostles (2:1–4).

When the day of Pentecost came, all the believers were gathered in one place. Suddenly there was a noise from the sky which sounded like a strong wind blowing, and it filled the whole house where they were sitting. Then they saw what looked like tongues as of fire which spread out and touched each person there. They were all filled with the Holy Spirit and began to talk in other languages, as the Spirit enabled them to speak.

The word of the Lord.

All: Thanks be to God.

Psalm Prayer (96:1-3, 10-13)

Psalm reader 1:

> Sing a new song to the Lord!
> Sing to the Lord, all the world!
> Sing to the Lord, and praise him!

All:　　　Sing a new song to the Lord!
　　　　　Sing to the Lord, all the world!

Psalm reader 2:

> Proclaim every day the good news that he has saved us.
> Proclaim his glory to the nations,
> his mighty deeds to all peoples.

All:　　　Sing a new song to the Lord!
　　　　　Sing to the Lord, all the world!

Psalm reader 3:

> Say to all the nations, "The Lord is king!
> The earth is set firmly in place and cannot be moved;
> he will judge the peoples with justice."

All:　　　Sing a new song to the Lord!
　　　　　Sing to the Lord, all the world!

Psalm reader 4:

> Be glad, earth and sky!
> Roar, sea, and every creature in you;
> be glad, fields, and everything in you!

All:　　　Sing a new song to the Lord!
　　　　　Sing to the Lord, all the world!

Psalm reader 5:

> The trees in the woods will shout for joy
> when the Lord comes to rule the earth.
> He will rule the peoples of the world
> with justice and fairness.

All: Sing a new song to the Lord!
        Sing to the Lord, all the world!

Gospel Reading

Gospel reader:

A reading from the holy gospel according to John
(14:25–27).

"I have told you this while I am still with you. The
Helper, the Holy Spirit, whom the Father will send in my
name, will teach you everything and make you
remember all that I told you. Peace is what I leave with
you; it is my own peace that I give you. I do not give it as
the world does. Do not be worried or upset; do not be
afraid."

The gospel of the Lord.

All: Praise to you, Lord Jesus Christ.

Intercessions

Leader: We pray that we may live the gifts of the Holy Spirit in
           our lives. Our response is: Spirit of God, come to us.

Reader 1: Bring us the gift of understanding, that we may know
           what is important in life.

All: Spirit of God, come to us.

Reader 2: Bring us the gift of wisdom, that we may share the good
           news of Jesus Christ.

All: Spirit of God, come to us.

Reader 3: Bring us the gift of wonder, that we may praise God in all
           that we do.

All: Spirit of God, come to us.

Reader 4:   Bring us the gift of respect, that we may see Jesus Christ in other people.

All: Spirit of God, come to us.

Reader 5:   Bring us the gift of right judgment, that we may make good choices in our lives.

All: Spirit of God, come to us.

Reader 6:   Bring us the gift of courage, that we may stand up for what is right,

All: Spirit of God, come to us.

Reader 7:   Bring us the gift of knowledge, that we may seek God's will in all things.

All: Spirit of God, come to us.

Closing Prayer

Make a Holy Spirit prayer card for each student. Type the closing prayer in fancy script. Add the outline of a dove and duplicate in red ink on white card stock. Six copies about 2″ by 5″ will fit on each page. Cut the duplicated prayers apart to create prayer cards. Put the prayer cards in a basket on the class prayer table.

holy Spirit Prayer

Come,
Holy Spirit,
direct my every
thought,
word, and
action

Leader:	Come forward now to get a Holy Spirit prayer card from the basket on our prayer table. We will pray this prayer together as our closing prayer. You may then keep the prayer card to take home. (Students take Holy Spirit card from the basket.) Let us pray.
All:	Come, Holy Spirit, direct my every thought, word, and action.

Closing Blessing

Leader:	We ask God's blessing on us. May, God who is the Father of us all, bless us in all that we do.
All:	Amen.
Leader:	May, God who is Son and Redeemer, bless us as we follow his way of love
All:	Amen.
Leader:	May, God who is the Spirit of love, bless us in service to others.
All:	Amen.

Greatest Commandment

Sharing With Others

Opening Prayer

Leader: Lord, we come before you today as your people. Open our hearts to your presence in our lives and in one another. Help us to see you in everyone we meet. Make us people of compassion, caring about others in your name.

All: Guide our lives that we may live in your way of love. Amen.

First Reading

Reader: A reading from the first letter of Peter (4:10–11).

Each one, as a good manager of God's different gifts, must use for the good of others the special gift he has received from God. Those who preach must preach God's message; those who serve must serve with the strength that God gives them, so that in all things praise may be given to God through Jesus Christ, to whom belong glory and power forever and ever. Amen.

The word of the Lord.

All: Thanks be to God.

Psalm Prayer (47:1-2, 5-8)

Reader: We now praise the Lord our God with our psalm.

Left: Clap your hands for joy, all peoples!
            Praise God with loud songs!

Right: The Lord, the Most High, is to be feared;
            he is a great king, ruling over all the world.

Left: God goes up to his throne.
            There are shouts of joy and the blast of trumpets
            as the Lord goes up.

Right: Sing praise to God;
            sing praise to our king!

Left: God is king over all the world;
            praise him with songs!

Right: God sits on his sacred throne;
            he rules over the nations.

Gospel Reading

Gospel reader:

Today we hear the call to live the greatest commandment. A reading from the holy gospel according to Mark (12:28–31).

A teacher of the Law was there who heard the discussion. He saw that Jesus had given the Sadducees a good answer, so he came to him with a question: "Which commandment is the most important of all?" Jesus replied, "The most important one is this: 'Listen Israel! The Lord our God is the only Lord. Love the Lord your God with all your heart, with all your soul, with all your mind, and with all your strength.' The second most important commandment is this: 'Love your neighbor as you love yourself.' There is no other commandment more important than these two."

The gospel of the Lord.

All: Praise to you, Lord Jesus Christ.

Family Place Collection

Collect items for a family place where family members stay while a child is treated at a local hospital. Send home a letter explaining the project and detailing a list of supplies needed. Items usually requested include food, such as breakfast cereal, cans of soup, and individual snacks; kitchen supplies such as paper plates and garbage bags; laundry supplies like laundry detergent and fabric softener; and personal care items including toothpaste, soap, and shampoo. (Check with the director of the facility to see if any other specific items may be needed.) Ask the students to decorate a box for the items they donate with the name of the organization.

Leader: If you were able to bring an item for the family place, please bring it forward at this time. We thank you for living the gospel and helping others. Remember these families in your prayers. (Students place their donations in the box.)

Prayers of Intercession

Leader: God of love, you call us to love others as ourselves. We come before you today with our prayers and petitions. Our response is: Lord, hear our prayer.

Reader 1:   May we live in love each day in all we do, we pray to the Lord.

All: Lord, hear our prayer.

Reader 2:   May our hearts be opened to the needs of others, we pray to the Lord.

All: Lord, hear our prayer.

Reader 3:	May we remember that Jesus came for all people, we pray to the Lord.
All:	Lord, hear our prayer.
Reader 4:	May we witness to what Jesus said and did in our lives, we pray to the Lord.
All:	Lord, hear our prayer.
Reader 5:	May we follow the Holy Spirit in all things, we pray to the Lord.
All:	Lord, hear our prayer.
Leader:	Thank you, God, for being here with us. We ask you to hear the prayers we have brought before you. Amen.

Closing Prayer

Leader:	We are called to share God's love with others. We must care about people of all nations, all races, and all religions. We should reach out to other people and follow the example of Jesus Christ.
All:	May we live with faith in the God of us all. May we hope in the peace of the Lord. May we love one another with the help of the Holy Spirit. Amen.

Living the Word of God

Opening Prayer

Leader: We gather together to hear the word of God and to offer prayers with one another. We are the people of God and are called to give glory to God's name.

All: May we listen to your Word and live it each day

Leader: God of all wisdom, open our hearts and minds to your presence in our lives and in one another. May we praise you in all we do.

All: Amen.

First Reading

Reader: A reading from the letter of Paul to the Colossians (1:9–10).

For this reason we have always prayed for you, ever since we heard about you. We ask God to fill you with the knowledge of his will, with all the wisdom and understanding that his Spirit gives. Then you will be able to live as the Lord wants and will always do what pleases him. Your lives will produce all kinds of good deeds, and you will grow in your knowledge of God.

The word of the Lord.

All: Thanks be to God.

Psalm Prayer (134)

Leader: Let us pray together our psalm prayer of praise to our God.

All: Come, praise the Lord, all his servants,
all who serve in his Temple at night.
Raise your hands in prayer in the Temple,
and praise the Lord!
May the Lord, who made heaven and earth,
bless you from Zion!

Gospel Reading

Gospel reader:

A reading about the sower from the holy gospel according to Mark (4:14–20).

The sower sows God's message. Some people are like the seeds that fall along the path; as soon as they hear the message, Satan comes and takes it away. Other people are like the seeds that fall on rocky ground. As soon as they hear the message, they receive it gladly. But it does not sink deep into them, and they don't last long. So when trouble or persecution comes because of the message, they give up at once. Other people are like the seeds sown among the thorn bushes. These are the ones who hear the message, but the worries about this life, the love for riches, and all other kinds of desires crowd in and choke the message, and they don't bear fruit. But other people are like seeds sown in good soil. They hear the message, accept it, and bear fruit.

The gospel of the Lord.

All: Praise to you, Lord Jesus Christ.

FALL WINTER SPRING SUMMER

Presentation of Bibles

Have a bible available for each student. These can be ordered at a bulk discount. Having their own bibles helps the students learn about God's word so they can live it.

Leader: Today we are presenting each of you with a bible so that you may learn about the word of God. May you grow in knowledge and faith in God's holy word, and live it in your lives. Please come forward for your bible at this time. (Students are each handed a bible.)

Intercessions

Leader: We are called to sow the seeds of God's Word in our world by what we say and do. We now pray together to our God, who is Lord of all. Our response is: Lord, hear our prayer.

Reader 1: May we sow seeds of hope, so that others may know the good news of Jesus Christ, we pray to the Lord.

All: Lord, hear our prayer.

Reader 2: May we sow seeds of justice, so that all people may be treated with respect and dignity, we pray to the Lord.

All: Lord, hear our prayer.

Reader 3: May we sow seeds of comfort, so that those who are suffering will be treated with compassion, we pray to the Lord.

All: Lord, hear our prayer.

Reader 4: May we sow seeds of forgiveness, so that people we forgive will by your example learn to forgive others, we pray to the Lord.

All: Lord, hear our prayer.

Reader 5: May we sow seeds of love, so that people will share with one another, we pray to the Lord.

All: Lord, hear our prayer.

Reader 6: May we sow seeds of peace, so that our world will know peace for all people and all nations, we pray to the Lord.

All: Lord, hear our prayer.

Our Father

Leader: Let us now pray together the prayer that Jesus taught us.

All: Our Father. . . .

Closing Prayer

Leader: Lord Jesus, you sow your word in our hearts and our lives. May our lives and our world be places where your word is heard. Help us witness to your word in all we say and do. May we live as people of faith, walk as people of hope, and grow as people of love.

All: May the word of God live in our hearts. Amen.

Closing Blessing

Leader: We ask God's blessing on us all in the name of the Father, the Son, and the Holy Spirit.

All: Amen.

Faith in God

Honoring St. Thomas

Opening Prayer

Leader: We celebrate today the faith of the apostle Thomas and our own faith in God. In the presence of the Lord Jesus Christ, we too are called to proclaim, "My Lord and My God!" He has redeemed us through his life, death, and resurrection.

All: Lord, give us faith that we may live as your disciples each day. Amen.

First Reading

Reader: A reading from the second letter to Timothy (1:9–10).

God saved us and called us to be his own people, not because of what we have done, but because of his own purpose and grace. He gave us this grace by means of Christ Jesus before the beginning of time, but now it has been revealed to us through the coming of our Savior, Christ Jesus.

The word of the Lord.

All: Thanks be to God

Psalm Prayer (66:1-5)

Psalm reader 1:

> Praise God with shouts of joy, all people!
> Sing to the glory of his name;
> offer him glorious praise!

All:　　　Come and see what God has done.

Psalm reader 2:

> Say to God, "How wonderful are the things you do!
> Your power is so great
> that your enemies bow down in fear before you.

All:　　　Come and see what God has done.

Psalm reader 3:

> Everyone on earth worships you;
> they sing praises to you,
> they sing praises to your name."

All:　　　Come and see what God has done.

Gospel Reading

(Before the prayer service, ask for volunteers to read the parts of the narrator, a disciple, Thomas, and Jesus. This dramatic reading brings the gospel alive for students.)

Narrator:　This is the story of Thomas from the gospel of John (20:24–31).

> One of the twelve disciples, Thomas (called the Twin), was not with them when Jesus came. So the other disciples told him,

Disciple:　"We have seen the Lord!"

Narrator:　Thomas said to them,

Thomas:	"Unless I see the scars of the nails in his hands and put my fingers on those scars and my hands in his side, I will not believe."
Narrator:	A week later his disciples were together again indoors, and Thomas was with them. The doors were locked, but Jesus came and stood among them and said,
Jesus:	"Peace be with you."
Narrator:	Then he said to Thomas,
Jesus:	"Put your finger here, and look at my hands; then reach out your hand and put it in my side. Stop your doubting, and believe!"
Narrator:	Thomas answered him,
Thomas:	"My Lord, and my God!"
Narrator:	Jesus said to him,
Jesus:	"Do you believe because you see me? How happy are those who believe without seeing me!"
Narrator:	In his disciples' presence Jesus performed many other miracles which are not written down in this book. But these have been written in order that you may believe that Jesus is the Messiah, the Son of God, and that through your faith in him you may have life.
	The gospel of the Lord.
All:	Praise to you, Lord Jesus Christ.

Intercessions

Leader:	As people of faith we bring our needs before the Lord. Our response is: Lord, hear our prayer.
Reader 1:	May we always have faith in the God who created us, redeemed us, and is with us always. We pray to the Lord.

All: Lord, hear our prayer.

Reader 2:   May we grow in love of God and others each day of our
            lives. We pray to the Lord.

All: Lord, hear our prayer

Reader 3:   May we be people of prayer who seek God's will in all
            things. We pray to the Lord.

All: Lord, hear our prayer.

Reader 4:   May we witness to the presence of the risen Christ in our
            lives by what we say and do. We pray to the Lord.

All: Lord, hear our prayer.

Reader 5:   May our hearts be open to the needs of others through
            the Holy Spirit. We pray to the Lord.

All: Lord, hear our prayer.

Leader: Lord Jesus Christ, Savior of the world, we ask you to hear
            our prayers.

All: Amen.

Closing Prayer

Leader: God, our Father, we pray that we may live our faith
            each day.
            May we be people of hope in all that we do and say.
            Help us to love you above all things and love others
            in your name.
            Be with us always that our lives may give you praise
            and glory.
            We ask this through your Son, Jesus Christ,
            and your Holy Spirit who guides our hearts and our lives.

All: Amen.

Hearts for Jesus

Caring About Others

Opening Prayer

Leader:　In the name of the Father who created us, the Son who redeemed us, and the Holy Spirit who lives in us.

All:　Amen.

Leader:　We gather together today to listen to the Word of God in scripture and to offer prayers to our God.

All:　Renew our hearts and our lives with your holy Word.

Leader:　God of all people, we come before you and remember that you call us to live in love with one another. In all he did and said, your Son, Jesus Christ, showed us how we are to live. Guide our lives in your way of love.

All:　May we walk in faith, hope, and love each day. Amen.

First Reading

Reader:　A reading from the letter of Paul to the Colossians (3:12–14).

You are the people of God; he loved you and chose you for his own. So then, you must clothe yourselves with compassion, kindness, humility, gentleness, and patience. Be tolerant with one another and forgive one another whenever any of you has a complaint against someone else. Your must forgive one another just as the Lord has forgiven you. And to all these qualities add love, which binds all things together in perfect unity.

The word of the Lord.

All: Thanks be to God.

Psalm Prayer (108:1-6)

Psalm reader 1:

I have complete confidence, O God!
I will sing and praise you!
Wake up, my soul!
Wake up, my harp and lyre!
I will wake up the sun.

All: I will thank you, O Lord, among the nations.
I will praise you among the peoples.

Psalm reader 2:

I will thank you, O Lord, among the nations.
I will praise you among the peoples.
Your constant love reaches above the heavens;
your faithfulness touches the skies.

All: I will thank you, O Lord, among the nations.
I will praise you among the peoples.

Psalm reader 3:

Show your greatness in the sky, O God,
and your glory over all the earth.
Save us by your might; answer my prayer.

All: I will thank you, O Lord, among the nations.
I will praise you among the peoples.

Gospel Reading

Gospel reader:

A reading from the holy gospel according to John (13:34–35).

"And now I give you a new commandment: love one another. As I have loved you, so you must love one another. If you have love for one another, then everyone will know you are my disciples."

The gospel of the Lord.

All: Praise to you, Lord Jesus Christ.

Hearts for Jesus

Before the prayer service provide duplicated red paper hearts with the words "Hearts for Jesus" for each of the students. On their hearts ask the students to write down something they will do to show love for others as Jesus taught us. They should bring their hearts for Jesus to the prayer service.

Leader: Please come forward now and place your heart for Jesus in the basket on our prayer table. Thank you for sharing the love of Jesus Christ with others through the action on your heart. (Allow students the opportunity to come forward.)

Intercessions

· ·

Leader: We now ask God to hear the prayers and petitions we offer. Our response is: Lord, hear our prayer.

Reader 1: Open our hearts to your love that others may know you through us.

All: Lord, hear our prayer.

Reader 2: Open our minds to your word that we may walk in faith.

All: Lord, hear our prayer.

Reader 3: Open our lives to your will that we may follow you each day.

All: Lord, hear our prayer.

Reader 4: Open our hands to serve others that we may help people in need.

All: Lord, hear our prayer.

Reader 5: Open our lives to your peace that we may live as peacemakers in our world.

All: Lord, hear our prayer.

Leader: God, Father of all people, we thank you for hearing our prayers. May we walk with Jesus Christ each day and serve others following his example. We ask this through your Spirit of love.

All: Amen.

Act of Love

Leader: Let us now pray together the Act of Love.

All: O my God,
I love you above all things, with my whole heart and soul,
because you are all good, worthy of all my love.
I love my neighbor as myself for love of you.
I forgive all who have injured me,
and I ask pardon of all whom I have injured. Amen.

Closing Prayer

Leader: Dear Jesus, you came to show us how to live in love. May we reach out to the poor, the homeless, the outcasts, the sick, and all people in need. We ask you to fill our hearts with love and our lives with service, all in your name.

All: Help us to live in God's love each day and to share that love with others. Amen.

Pray Always

Giving Thanks and Praise to God

Opening Prayer

Leader: We gather together to give praise and thanks to our God. Our God is a loving, merciful God who created us and everything in our world. We were made to give glory to God in all that we do and say.

All: God, hear our prayers that we bring before you.

Leader: Prayer is an important part of our relationship with God. Prayer helps us to remember that everything we have and everything we are comes from God. We are to pray as Jesus showed us, with the help of the Holy Spirit.

All: God, help us to be people of prayer in all things. Amen.

First Reading

Reader: A reading from the book of Numbers (6:24–26).
May the Lord bless you and take care of you;
May the Lord be kind and gracious to you;
May the Lord look upon you with favor and
give you peace.

The word of the Lord.

All: Thanks be to God.

Psalm Prayer (34:1-4)

Leader: Let us give praise to God by praying our psalm.

Left: I will always thank the Lord;
I will never stop praising him.

Right: I will praise him for what he has done;
may all who are oppressed listen and be glad!

Left: Proclaim with me the Lord's greatness;
let us praise his name together!

Right: I prayed to the Lord, and he answered me;
he freed me from all my fears.

Gospel Reading

Gospel reader:

A reading from the holy gospel according to Matthew
(6:9–13).

"This, then, is how you should pray:
Our Father in heaven:
May your holy name be honored;
may your Kingdom come;
may your will be done on earth as it is in heaven.,
Give us today the food we need.
Forgive us the wrongs we have done,
as we forgive the wrongs that others have done to us.
Do not bring us to hard testing,
but keep us safe from the Evil One."

The gospel of the Lord

All: Praise to you, Lord Jesus Christ.

Prayer Chain

· ·

During class talk about the importance of praying for the needs of other people. Discuss some of the people who need our prayers, such as the sick, the poor, and the homeless. Let the students make a class prayer chain with prayers for others. Have the students cut strips of colorful construction paper lengthwise. On each strip they should print a petition such as, "I pray for the hungry," or "I pray for my Grandma who is sick." Each student may make several prayer links. All of the prayer links of the students are joined together in one long chain using tape. Display the prayer chain in the area where the prayer service is held.

Intercessions

· ·

Leader: We pray for people in need in our world. Our response is: Lord, hear our prayer.

Reader 1:   For people who go to bed hungry, for those who do not have clean drinking water, and for those who live in areas suffering from famine, we pray to the Lord.

All: Lord, hear our prayer.

Reader 2:   For people who live in countries torn apart by war, for victims of land mines, and for those who live each day in fear, we pray to the Lord.

All: Lord, hear our prayer.

Reader 3:   For people who are homeless on the streets, for the families of those in jail, and for people who are lonely, we pray to the Lord.

All: Lord, hear our prayer.

Reader 4:   For people who are sick and in the hospital, for those who do not have access to medical care, and for those who are mentally ill, we pray to the Lord.

All: Lord, hear our prayer.

Reader 5: For the people on our class prayer chain and for all those who are in need around the world, we pray to the Lord.

All: Lord, hear our prayer.

Our Father

Leader: Let us now pray together the prayer that Jesus gave us.

All: Our Father. . . .

Closing Prayer

Leader: We are called to follow the example of Jesus and be people of prayer. Prayer helps us to lift up our hearts and our lives to God who is the Father of us all. Prayer should be a part of everything we do.

All: God, Father and Creator, help us to remember to pray each day for our needs and the needs of other people. We ask this through your Son, Jesus Christ, and the Holy Spirit. Amen.

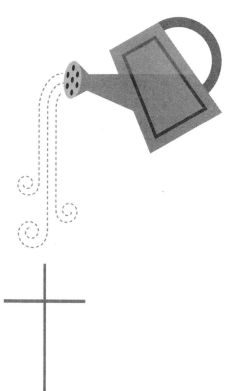

Walk in Justice

Loving Others

Opening Prayer

Leader: Jesus, you call us to live in justice in our communities and in the world.

All: May we work for the rights of all people.

Leader: Help us to remember that each person is created in God's image and likeness.

All: May we treat everyone with respect.

Leader: Jesus, you challenge us to be people of justice and love.

All: May we speak for those who are oppressed and reach out to the poor.

Leader: Help us to live as people of your kingdom in all that we do.

All: May we be people of justice and love.

First Reading

Reader: A reading from the book of Micah (6:8).

The Lord has told us what is good. What he requires of us is this: to do what is just, to show constant love, and to live in humble fellowship with our God.

The word of the Lord.

All: Thanks be to God.

Psalm Prayer (106:1-3, 47-48)

Leader: We give thanks to God with our psalm.

Left: Praise the Lord!
            Give thanks to the Lord, because he is good,
            his love is eternal.

Right: Who can tell all the great things he has done?
            Who can praise him enough?
            Happy those who obey his commands,
            who always do what is right.

Left: Save us, O Lord our God,
            and bring us back from among the nations,
            so that we may be thankful
            and praise your holy name.

Right: Praise the Lord, the God of Israel;
            praise him now and forever!

            Let everyone say, "Amen!" Praise the Lord!

Gospel Reading

Gospel reader:

            A reading from the holy gospel according to Luke
            (10:30–34, 36–37).

Jesus answered,

            "There was once a man who was going down from
            Jerusalem to Jericho when robbers attacked him, stripped
            him, and beat him up, leaving him half dead. It so
            happened that a priest was going down the road; but
            when he saw the man, he walked on by on the other
            side. In the same way a Levite also came there, went

over and looked at the man, and then walked on by on the other side. But a Samaritan who was traveling that way came upon the man, and when he saw him, his heart was filled with pity. He went over to him, poured oil and wine on his wounds and bandaged them; then he put the man on his own animal and took him to an inn, where he took care of him. . . ." And Jesus concluded, "In your opinion, which one of these three acted like a neighbor toward the man attacked by the robbers?" The teacher of the Law answered, "The one who was kind to him." Jesus replied, "You go, then, and do the same."

The gospel of the Lord.

All: Praise to you, Lord Jesus Christ.

Reaching Out to Refugees

Refugee families are forced to start their lives over again due to war and violence in their home country. They have to leave everything behind when they flee to safety. These families have a great need for basic household furnishings. There are agencies and churches who strive to help refugee families get resettled, but they need our donations. Encourage students and their families to reach out and lend a helping hand. Basic items needed by refugee families include dishes, pots and pans, coffee pots, glasses, can openers, dish towels, bakeware, silverware, sheets, blankets, pillows, alarm clocks, lamps, and bath towels. A class can collect items for a specific room in the house such as the kitchen, bedroom, or bathroom. Provide a marked box for donations in the area where the prayer service is held. (If your parish is not involved with refugees, contact another parish that is or call your diocesan Catholic Charities office for a referral.)

Leader: At this time I invite you to bring forward the items you have for our refugee families. Thank you for reaching out a helping hand to refugees in our community. Please remember them in your prayers as they begin a new life.

Intercessions:

. . . .

Leader: We pray that we may make the world a better place for all nations, all races, all people. Our response is: Jesus, help us to walk in justice.

Reader 1:   May we live the gospel each day in all that we do, in all that we say, and in all that we are.

All: Jesus, help us to walk in justice.

Reader 2:   May we put God first in our lives and in our hearts, and turn away from selfishness.

All: Jesus, help us to walk in justice.

Reader 3:   May we treat all people with dignity and respect, and work for an end to violence and hatred.

All: Jesus, help us to walk in justice.

Reader 4:   May we follow God's will even when it is difficult and share God's love with everyone we meet.

All: Jesus, help us to walk in justice.

Reader 5:   May we live in peace and reach out a hand of friendship to people of all nations and races.

All: Jesus, help us to walk in justice.

Leader: We ask you, Lord, to hear our prayers and petitions this day. Amen.

Closing Prayer

. . . .

Leader: Father, you are the creator of all things and all people. You sent Jesus Christ to show us how to live in justice and reach out to others in your name. May we work for justice for all people in our world.

All: Amen.

Gospel Story Prayer Service

Matthew

Matthew 2:1, 9–11	Star	Journey of the Wise Men
Matthew 5:23–24	Make Peace	Live in Peace
Matthew 6:9–13	Our Father	Pray Always
Matthew 16:13–18	Peter	You are the Messiah
Matthew 19:16–22	Rich Man	Give to Others
Matthew 25:34–40	Feed Hungry	Works of Mercy
Matthew 28:1–2, 5–6	Mary Magdalene	Signs of Easter
Matthew 28:18–20	Baptize	Patron of Ireland

Mark

Mark 1:4–5, 7–9	John the Baptist	Waiting for Jesus
Mark 1:14–15	Kingdom	Renew our Hearts
Mark 4:13–20	The Sower	Sowing Seeds
Mark 9:33–35	Servant of All	The Little Flower
Mark 10:42–45	Serve	Live in Hope
Mark 12:28–31	Love God	Greatest Commandment

Luke

Luke 1:26–38	Mary	Annunciation of the Lord
Luke 2:8–16	Shepherds	Glory to God
Luke 6:37	Do Not Judge	Life of Love
Luke 9:23–25	The Cross	Take up Your Cross
Luke 10:30–34, 36–37	Good Samaritan	Walk in Justice
Luke 15:11–14, 17–24	Prodigal Son	God of Mercy
Luke 18:35–43	Blind Man	Believe in Jesus Christ
Luke 24:13–35	Two Disciples	Road to Emmaus

John

John 1:1–4	The Word	Give Thanks to God
John 8:12	Light	Light of the World
John 13:34–35	Love One Another	Hearts for Jesus
John 14:18–21	Commandments	Honor the Saints
John 14:25–27	Holy Spirit	Living in the Spirit
John 20:24–31	Thomas	Faith in God

Patricia Mathson, a leader in religious education for over twenty-three years, is Director of Religious Education at Holy Trinity Catholic Church in Des Moines, Iowa. She served previously in a similar position in two parishes in Texas.

The author of eight books on creative approaches to catechesis and prayer, Mathson writes regularly for *Catechist* and *Religion Teacher's Journal.* Her most recent books are: *Bless This Day: 150 Everyday Prayers for Grades 1-5* and *Bundles of Faith and Tons of Fun: Easy Activities, Prayers and Projects for Children* (Ave Maria Press).